AGING WITH PURPOSE

Seven Essentials for Finishing Well

Hal Habecker

With *Philip Rawley*

Copyright © 2023 – Finishing Well Ministries

All rights to this book are reserved. No permission is given for any part of this book to be reproduced, transmitted in any form or means; electronic or mechanical, stored in a retrieval system, photocopied, recorded, scanned, or otherwise. Any of these actions require the proper written permission of the author.

"Fulfilling God's Plan in Our Aging Years"

"Finishing Well Ministries aims to encourage every retired Christian and every Christian thinking about retirement to understand and to fully live out God's plan for these critically important years."

www.FinishingWellMinistries.org

Printed by Finishing Well Ministries

Printed in the United States of America
First Printing Edition, 2023

DEDICATION

Special thanks to my wife, Vicki, whose support,
and inspiration make living well and
finishing well a constant joy.

ACKNOWLEDGEMENTS & THANKS

The Finishing Well Ministries' Board
who makes this ministry possible.

Rankin Gasaway
Randy Hess
Steve Parish
Brent Ratliff
Link Simpson

-

Chip Mansfield
Ministry Support

-

Cover Design by Jim Foley
www.loudthought.com

Table of Contents

Introduction.. vii

Chapter ONE: The First Essential
      The Importance of Growing 1

Chapter TWO: The Second Essential:
      The Importance of Connecting.......... 23

Chapter THREE: The Third Essential
      The Importance of Caring/Loving.... 43

Chapter FOUR: The Fourth Essential
      The Importance of Investing
      In Younger Generations................... 59

Chapter FIVE: The Fifth Essential
      The Importance of Being Available...... 79

Chapter SIX: The Sixth Essential
      The Importance of Planning Ahead
      for When We Will Not Be Here............. 93

Chapter SEVEN: The Seventh Essential
      The Importance of
      Anticipating Heaven................... 111

Bibliography... 123

INTRODUCTION

In his wonderful poem, *Rabbi Ben Ezra*, Robert Browning expressed the delight that awaits us when we approach our aging years in joyful anticipation of what God has for us in this important time of life. It has become something of a theme for this ministry:

> Grow old along with me!
>
> The best is yet to be,
>
> The last of life, for which the first was made:
>
> Our times are in His hand
>
> Who saith, "A whole I planned,
>
> Youth shows but half"; trust God: see all, nor be afraid."

The apostle Paul certainly understood this. I have always been greatly challenged and motivated by his assessment of his ministry as he neared the end of his life:

> *For I am already being poured out as a drink offering, and the time of my departure has come. I have fought the good fight, I have finished the course, I have kept the faith; in the future there is laid up for me the crown of righteousness, which the Lord, the righteous Judge, will award to me on that day; and not only to me, but also to all who have loved His appearing.* 2 Timothy 4.6–8

Introduction

These are the words of a follower of Christ who finished well! I've read and taught this remarkable passage a number of times as a pastor for 21 years and a teacher of God's Word for over 45 years. But as I moved toward and am now well into what our culture calls the retirement years, Paul's testimony of a life well lived for Christ began to take on a whole new meaning.

The apostle's words expressed what I wanted to accomplish for the Lord, for my family, and for the church of Jesus Christ in my aging years. I wanted to finish my race well, which has led me on an amazing adventure since 2015 when I founded ***Finishing Well Ministries.***

We often hear it said that the word "retirement" is not in the Bible (except for Numbers 8.23-26, but this was a very special case). It's true, because we don't retire from being Christians, and Jesus doesn't put any age limit on His command to share the Gospel and make disciples (Matthew 28.18–20). There's nothing wrong with capping years of service in a job or with a company and looking forward to spending more time with family and friends, and doing things we always wanted to do but didn't have time for.

But retirement as we practice it today is a social and cultural construct, not a biblical one, which means that it comes with all sorts of assumptions that work against the biblical concept of finishing well.

For example, to most people retirement means the end of their productive years. Their careers are over. In many cases, they no longer have input in the field, or fields, where they spent so many years, and they may be made to feel that their

Introduction

ideas are no longer welcome. They have nothing to offer. They've run their race, so to speak, and now it's time to pass the baton to the next generation and sit back with nothing to do.

And the advertisers will make sure that seniors and retirees buy into the idea that the years ahead of them are for nothing but travel, entertainment, and leisure.

There's nothing wrong with these pursuits, but as disciples of Jesus Christ we are called to so much more. The Bible presents us with wonderful examples of people who accomplished great things for God in their "golden years."

Moses was 80 years old when God called him to lead two million Israelites out of slavery in Egypt to the Promised Land—and Moses led them for another 40 years! Caleb was 85 when he said to Joshua in the Promised Land:

> *Now behold, the LORD has let me live, just as He spoke, these forty-five years, from the time that the LORD spoke this word to Moses, when Israel walked in the wilderness; and now behold, I am eighty-five years old today. I am still as strong today as I was in the day Moses sent me; as my strength was then, so my strength is now, for war and for going out and coming in. Now then, give me this hill country about which the LORD spoke on that day.* Joshua 14.10–12

What an amazing testimony! We also read that Joseph died at the age of 110 (Genesis 50.22), still presumably

Introduction

leading the nation of Egypt into which he had been sold as a teenager.

The more I studied what the Bible says about aging and God's purposes for His people, the more I realized that the only "expiration date" on Jesus' call to me to be His disciple, teach His Word, love people, and help mentor the next generation is when my work is finished, and He takes me to heaven. Until then, I'm to fulfill God's will and purposes for me every day and in every stage of life.

Think about this statement from Paul in light of our aging years: *"The gifts and the calling of God are irrevocable"* (Romans 11.29). This means that God hasn't changed His mind and pulled my discipleship papers. So even if I wanted to drop out of the race of the Christian life and tell God, "I've run my lap and handed off the baton. It's somebody else's turn to run," God's response would be, "No, you're still in the race. You may not be as fast as you used to be, but I want you to stay in there."

Now don't misunderstand. As a 70-something walking on an ankle rebuilt with a metal scaffold, I know how much things change as we age. You may be experiencing diminished physical strength and mobility, serious health issues, family crises, or financial challenges.

These things are real, but the point is not what you and I *can't* do, but what we *can* do with the minds, bodies, and resources God has given us at this stage of our lives. And my friend, I'm discovering that we can do a lot! I have friends in their 80s and 90s who are defying the odds, as the world might

Introduction

say, and going strong for the Lord, having as much impact for the church and the gospel today as they've ever had.

We've been hearing for years that we Baby Boomers, who are retiring at the rate of 10,000 *per day*, are the largest untapped source of ability, experience, wisdom—and even manpower—in history. There are millions of us, including millions sitting in our churches every Sunday thinking, rightly or wrongly, that the church doesn't need them and has no place for them to serve.

Nothing could be farther from the truth! And the more I realized the exciting plans God has to use us in our aging years, the more excited I got about that potential and what I could to help mobilize seniors for His work. But I also realized that for this to happen, we needed to change the way our society, and even the church, thinks about aging.

That's how God led me to launch FWM, an ambitious initiative to change the narrative about aging people in the life of our churches and communities. We see the presence of aging followers of Christ as a growing convoy or "peloton" (a bike rider's term I'll explain as we go) of saints purposing to make a greater difference for Christ throughout their aging years. That legacy will strengthen the work of Christ for future generations.

The mission of FWM is to strengthen the ways Christians **think about** and **live in** retirement. As I said above, culturally speaking, retirement means that we stop working at a certain age and begin receiving Social Security. Most retires seem to understand that this new season means that we step back, embrace a life of leisure, travel at will, and/or see the world.

Introduction

At that point life changes. Purpose changes. *Or purpose may be lacking.*

Thinking biblically, however, as followers of Christ, we are called to keep growing spiritually, to keep being conformed to the image of Christ, to keep building the church, to keep sharing the Gospel, to keep on being ambassadors for Christ, to keep using our giftedness, to keep being filled with the Spirit, and to keep on making disciples in ***every one*** of our retirement years. Mobilizing seniors throughout their retirement years for His purposes is our purpose

To encourage this biblical mindset in retirement is the purpose of FWM's *7 Essentials for Finishing Well* discipleship project, of which this book is a summary. **FWM** has developed a video series/workbook to focus on these essentials in life that will help us live well and finish well. The series is designed with retired and aging people in mind, so I hope this book will whet your appetite to learn more. You can find the series at *finishingwellministries.org*.

I pray that this book will encourage you to purpose to finish well, so that your life will bear witness to our Lord Jesus Christ. Before you turn the page, consider these words from the late, tremendous Christian leader and Bible teacher, Dr. J. I. Packer:

> *Runners in a distance race ... always try to keep something in reserve for a final sprint. And my contention is that, so far as our bodily health allows, we should aim to be found running the last lap of the race of our Christian life, as we would say, flat out. The*

Introduction

final sprint, so I urge, should be a sprint indeed. (Finishing Our Course with Joy, pp. 21–22)

If after reading this book, you would like to explore the Seven Essentials more deeply, you may go to our website for the full video series and accompanying study guide. Visit www.finishingwellministries.org.

*All Scriptural references are from the NASB Updated Version of the Bible. For clarity, we have also italicized all Scripture quotes, and all **bold words** are our emphasis. @ Copyright by Finishing Well Ministries, 2023.)*

CHAPTER ONE

The First Essential
The Importance of Growing

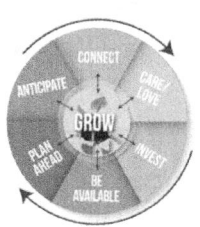

"Old age is as important and meaningful a part of God's perfect will as youth. He is interested in both the waxing and waning of life. Just as potential is locked up in young people and often never developed, so the full possibilities of old age often remain dormant and die with a person. The work of God will be greatly enriched when more attention is given to releasing and utilizing hidden this hidden resource."
- The late Dr. Howard Hendricks, Former Professor at Dallas Theological Seminary

I love this quote by one of my former mentors and a beloved professor at my alma mater. It expresses so well the goal of this book and the purpose behind FWM. You'll meet Dr. Hendricks again in a later chapter because his life was a godly example of what it means to finish well, and his teaching was a fountain of wisdom from which thousands of students at DTS drank, me included.

The *Seven Essentials for Finishing Well* begin with **GROWTH**, which I believe is the foundation on which everything else is built, as this illustration shows:

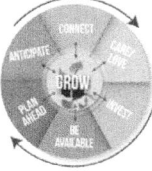

But it's possible that just mentioning the word "growth" in our aging years may conjure up negative or even funny images in your mind. For example, any physical growth we experience in our later years is usually in places where we don't *want* to grow.

We've all heard the jokes; we men talk about carrying around a spare tire, not being able to see our feet when we stand up or having "dunlap disease" because our belly has "done lapped" over our belt. And just so no one feels left out, one little boy declared authoritatively that all grandmas are "fat." We'll leave that one right there!

This is not a book about eating right or taking care of our bodies as we age, although these things are important. And I want to acknowledge up front that nothing said in the following pages is meant to ignore or minimize the toll that diminished strength, energy, and chronic or even debilitating physical conditions can take on our bodies and minds. That's why you need to read this material through the lens of your situation and adjust as necessary.

We're going to concentrate on other areas of growth where age need not be a deterrent—growing and maturing emotionally, relationally, intellectually (in terms of learning), and most importantly, spiritually. I added "maturing" because the fact is that simply growing older does not automatically mean that we are growing more mature and wiser than we were earlier in life. What we are going to study in this book takes effort and attention on our part.

But before we plunge into this study, I want to address what we might call "the elephant in the room," which is the attitude that says, "No thanks" to this idea that growing is a goal we should have in our aging years. I realize that some, perhaps many, seniors approach life with the attitude that they have done their time and paid their dues, so the only thing they want to pursue is their leisure and pleasure. These people might believe that growing and changing in their latter years is optional, and they pass on that option.

If you're tempted to think this way, consider that growing in every stage of life is not an option that we can reject with no consequences, but part of our calling in Christ Jesus. Here is a list of the negative results of failing to grow as seniors that we agreed upon in one of the seminars I teach on the seven essentials. We asked, "What does the lack of growth look like at this stage of our lives?" Here are some answers:

- Feeling of uselessness
- Disappointment
- Bitterness
- Anger
- Selfishness, self-centeredness, absorbed with self
- Laziness
- Narcissism
- No expectations
- Stagnation
- Deterioration
- No real sense of purpose/mission

I don't believe these are the negative qualities you want your life to reflect, or you wouldn't have picked up this book. So, let's get started.

Lifelong Process

It's a truism to say that God designed us to grow, just as He designed all of His creation to grow. Growth is at the core of life. We are hard-wired for growth in our marriages, families, businesses if that applies, and in our relationship with Jesus Christ as His disciples (a word that means "learner," as we'll see below).

As parents, we wanted our children to grow, and we celebrated each stage of that growth. Now, we do the same with our grandchildren and great-grandchildren. Children are born to grow, and so are adults. Growing is a lifelong process that is never finished until we are no longer here.

But the fallacy built into our society's concept of aging is that once you reach that magic plateau called retirement, you can stop growing and start coasting because your productive years are behind you. You've earned your leisure, so the only thing left is to take your ease, "eat, drink and be merry" as the foolish farmer in Jesus' parable said (Luke 12.19).

We can clearly see this concept of retirement in the athletic world. When a pro athlete retires, he quits doing what he loves and usually fades away in people's memories. If he was a great basketball player, for example, the team may hang his jersey from the rafters and talk about him in the past tense, as if he were dead! Most people just get the proverbial gold watch and retirement luncheon as a sendoff. This is our culture's idea of aging, which we must fight.

God has called us to so much more in this season of our lives. Some of the most meaningful growth, productive years, satisfying relationships, and spiritual impact can come in our 60s, 70, 80s, and even 90s. God calls us to keep growing, even in our aging years.

Biblical Examples of Aging Well

I love the Bible's examples of this truth. Abraham received the promise of a son when he was 75, and yet Isaac wasn't born until Abraham was 100. But those years of waiting were a period of spiritual growth for Abraham because he *"grew strong in faith"* (Romans 4.20), despite his and Sarah's advanced age.

Moses was 80 years old when God called him to lead the Israelites out of Egypt. That story is well-chronicled in Scripture; Moses also wrote Psalm 90, the oldest psalm in the book. The words of verse 12 are familiar to many of us, but they take on extra meaning when you realize that they were written by an aging and aged saint: *"So **teach** (help us learn/grow) us to number our days, that we may present to You a heart of wisdom."*

This is a clarion call to us to keep growing every day of our lives. Notice that the goal of this growing process is wisdom, the ability to apply the knowledge God gives us to every area and circumstance of life. That's important because wisdom comes from growth and maturity, not just from the passing of years. In other words, it's not automatic. We've all heard the expression, "There's no fool like an old fool." Moses didn't want to end his life as an old fool!

The apostle Paul was in his 60s, *and in prison*, when he wrote that he was pressing on in his life and ministry because he had not yet attained the prize of Christ's "well done":

> *Not that I have already obtained it or have already become perfect, but **I press** (pursue) on so that I may lay hold of that for which also I was laid hold of by Christ Jesus. Brethren, I do not regard myself as having laid hold of it yet; but one thing I do: forgetting what lies behind and **reaching forward** to what lies ahead, **I press** (pursue) on toward the goal for the prize of the upward call of God in Christ Jesus.* Philippians 3.12–14

The word "press" that Paul uses here means "to flee," "put to flight" "persecute," or "pursue." While the word is generally used of a desperate action in a negative situation, here the word is used in a positive sense. Paul was deeply intentional and purposeful about growing in his life, pressing on. There is nothing casual about the action. He was desperate about growing in Christ, and about pursuing the mission Jesus had for him.

This helps us understand why Paul also wrote the verses below. While there are plenty of potential physical hardships in life as we age, Paul did not allow these things to deter him from his God-given life mission:

> *Therefore, we do not lose heart, but though our outer man is decaying, yet our inner man is **being renewed day by day**. For momentary, light affliction is producing for us an eternal weight of glory far beyond all comparison, while we look not at the things which are seen, but at the things which are not seen; for the things which are seen are temporal, but the things which are not seen are eternal.* 2 Corinthians 4.16–18

Elsewhere Paul described the goal of this daily renewal: *"For those whom He foreknew, He also predestined to become **conformed** to the image of His Son, so that He would be the firstborn among many brethren"* (Romans 8.29). As in all of these verses about the challenge of growing as Christ's followers, there is no age limit on this. No matter how long we live, God's desire is that we keep on growing more and more into the image of Christ.

The apostle Peter stated the goal of growth very directly. Also in his 60s, he wrote in his final letter:

> *For if these qualities are yours and are **increasing**, they render you neither useless nor unfruitful in the true knowledge of our Lord Jesus Christ. For he who lacks these qualities is blind or short-sighted, having forgotten his purification from his former sins.* 2 Peter 1.8–9

Peter had listed these qualities in verses 5–7, exhorting his readers to diligently add these seven traits to their lives. And then, Peter's last words are a stirring challenge to all of us in our aging years: *"But **grow** in the grace and knowledge of our*

Lord and Savior Jesus Christ. To Him be the glory, both now and to the day of eternity. Amen." (2 Peter 3.18).

Of course, the greatest example of someone who grew throughout his life is Jesus Christ. He *"grew in wisdom and stature, and in favor with God and men"* (Luke 2.52). During His earthly life Jesus grew intellectually, physically, socially, and spiritually. That's an amazing statement. The Bible also says that Jesus *"learned obedience from the things which He suffered"* (Hebrews 5.8)

We want to grow in understanding what is expected in our maturity process in life. Are we growing in wisdom, education, relationships, work, and in the work of life? Are we growing in our marriages, our families, or in our community of faith?

God designed us to grow. He calls us to keep growing. Our aging years call to us to grow. This simple graphic captures the idea of getting out of bed each morning with a mission in mind to keep growing.

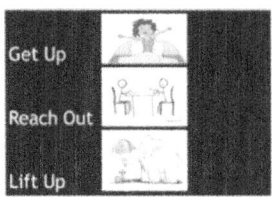

More Thoughts on Growth

Jesus called His followers "disciples," a word that means "learner" or "pupil." Jesus told His followers, *"A pupil is not above his teacher; but everyone, after he has been fully trained, will be like his teacher"* (Luke 6.40).

Jesus has a training process, a growing process, for every one of His followers. Each day provides new opportunities to learn and grow. In this aging season of our lives, we have countless opportunities to learn how God is calling us to grow and what He wants us to be.

There is an adage about fishing that says; "You never fish in the same river twice." The river is always changing. That's true of life as well. Each day is different than the day before. We ourselves are different. With each new day God keeps giving us the opportunity to grow.

Life is about change. Every day and each new season of life brings change; physically, spiritually, emotionally, and mentally. Generally speaking, though, we tend to resist change as we age. Change isn't always easy, as the Russian novelist Leo Tolstoy acknowledged: "Everybody thinks of changing humanity and nobody thinks of changing himself."

Yet Jesus Himself calls us to keep learning and growing in order to become more like Him. Paul said that God has saved and called us to be "*conformed to the image of His Son [Jesus]*" (Romans 8.29). But does this mean we have to just overlook all of the challenges and limitations of aging and push ourselves constantly to the edge of exhaustion?

Of course not. Every principle I've developed in this study of finishing well attempts to take these factors into account. Jesus knows how He made us and what we can do. He made a wonderful promise that I believe has special meaning to those of us who are aging:

*Come to Me, all who are weary and heavy-laden, and I will give you rest. Take My yoke upon you and **learn** from Me, for I am gentle and humble in heart, **and you will find rest for your souls**. For My yoke is easy and My burden is light.* Matthew 11.28–30

Notice what this passage does and does *not* say. This is not a call to kick back and coast through the rest of our lives. Jesus knows we get weary, and He promises to provide the rest that He knows we need. But note that this rest is in the context of taking Jesus' "yoke," which is the work He has given us to accomplish for our good and His glory.

A yoke implies work, effort. But the work Jesus has for us is meaningful and rewarding, not just plowing a rut. It's our calling to follow Jesus as His disciples who need to learn from Him every day. I hope you know the feeling of doing something you love so much that even when you are hard at it, you are refreshed by it. That's what Jesus is talking about.

Pastor and author Alistair Begg said: "Are we willing to learn and grow from Jesus in every area of our lives? Do you see learning of Jesus as a privilege, and not a burden, to follow His teaching and place ourselves under His authority? Let's seize every opportunity to learn and grow gospel truth, and may it satisfy our heart's longings and transform your life day by day."

Paul captured this idea well as he likened the Christian life to a race. Paul wanted to keep running and reaching forward to the finish line because he had a great prize waiting for him.

> *Do you not know that those who run in a race all run, but only one receives the prize? Run in such a way that you may win. Everyone who competes in the games exercises self-control in all things. They then do it to receive a perishable wreath, but we an imperishable. Therefore I run in such a way, as not without aim; I box in such a way, as not beating the air.* 1 Corinthians 9.24–27

The word "competes" means that the athlete is caught up in the struggle, expending energy to keep running toward the finish line. Life for Paul was not a "walk in the park" in his later years. That's why he would say at the end of his life's race, *"I have finished the course"* (2 Timothy 4.7). There are no awards for runners who quit in the last lap of the race.

John Stott, the late Anglican pastor and Bible scholar, likened our need for continual spiritual growth to having a healthy appetite, even in our aging years:

> There is perhaps no greater secret of progress in Christian living than in a healthy, hearty spiritual appetite. Again and again, Scripture addresses its promises to the hungry. God 'satisfied him who is thirsty, and the hungry he fills with good things' (Psalm 107.9). If we are conscious of slow growth, is the reason that we have a jaded appetite? It is not enough to mourn over past sin; we must also hunger for future righteousness. (*Authentic Christianity*, # 481, "A Hearty Appetite")

The above Scriptures and the theme of growth go against the drift of our culture. "To retire" literally means "to stop" or "to disengage." When one "retires," we stop going to work. Our economic productivity stops. When we "retire" for the day, we usually go to sleep.

To the contrary of our cultural pattern, I want to continue growing in Christ every day of my life. I want to be continually ambitious to keep serving Him. That's why I advocate a different perspective. *We as believers will not become conformed to this world of retirement* (Romans 12.2).

In all of life, it is very empowering to recognize that we have some control of what we eat, how we choose to exercise, what we believe spiritually, how we exercise our faith, and how socially engaged we are in helping others and living life courageously. But all of these require growth.

We also want to keep growing to become more self-aware as individuals. Understanding your giftedness, weaknesses, and personal tendencies is a never-ending growth process.

Growing through Life's Challenges

As we think about the issue of growing during our latter years and all the challenges it presents, I'm reminded of the statement I've heard often that doing something beneficial or healthful isn't always easy. If it were easy, everybody would do it. But it still needs to be done to gain the benefits. That's true of growing at our stage of life.

This is why I believe our greatest growth may come through the most difficult challenges, whatever they may be. Whether these are aging challenges/hardships, or just the general challenges/hardships of life, we can grow through them.

There is no denying that the aging of our bodies often brings new hardships. Paul recognized the need to prepare for this season and put it into perspective:

> *Therefore, we do not lose heart, but though our outer man is decaying, yet our inner man is being renewed day by day. For momentary, light affliction is producing for us an eternal weight of glory far beyond all comparison, while we look not at the things which are seen, but at the things which are not seen; for the things which are seen are temporal, but the things which are not seen are eternal.* 2 Corinthians 4.16–18

Francois Fenelon, the seventeenth-century theologian and writer, said this about the importance of growing through life's challenges:

Embrace the difficult circumstances you find yourself in, even when you feel they will overwhelm you. Allow God to mold you through the events He allows to enter your life. This will make you flexible toward the will of God. The events of life are like a furnace for the heart. All your impurities are melted and your old ways are lost. The intrusions that God sends you will no doubt upset your plans and oppose all that you want. But they will chase you towards God. Francois Fenelon, *The Seeking Heart*, Seed Sowers Publishing, p.14 (Quoted also in *The Softer Side of Leadership: Essentials Soft Skills That Transform Leaders and the People They Lead*, Eugene Habecker, p.100).

We saw above that even Jesus grew through His suffering, as hard as that may seem for us to grasp given that He is the perfect Son of God. But the Scriptures are clear on this point. Jesus learned and *kept growing* through His difficulties. The book of Hebrews has some key passages about Jesus' suffering and learning that we can learn from:

But we do see Him who was made for a little while lower than the angels, namely, ***Jesus****, because of the suffering of death crowned with glory and honor, so that by the grace of God He might taste death for everyone. For it was fitting for Him, for whom are all things, and through whom are all things, in bringing many sons to glory,* ***to perfect the author of their salvation through sufferings.*** Hebrews 2.9–10

Therefore, since we have so great a cloud of witnesses surrounding us, let us also lay aside every encumbrance and the sin which so easily entangles us, and let us run with endurance the race that is set before us, ***fixing our eyes on Jesus****, the author and perfecter of faith, who for the joy set before Him endured the cross, despising the shame, and has sat down at the right hand of the throne of God.* ***For consider Him who has endured such hostility by***

sinners against Himself, so that you will not grow weary and lose heart. Hebrews 12.1–3

Jesus grew to the very end of His life and finished His mission, His death on the cross. We can learn the value of endurance from His example—embracing our hardships instead of becoming angry, bitter, or discouraged over them—because we know that God is working through them for our growth and benefit. Jesus had a mission to glorify His Father and secure our salvation, and He let nothing deter Him from accomplishing it.

Your Mission

Do you have a life mission statement? Do you have a purpose in life that gets you up every morning and spurs you to keep growing? If you do not have a well-thought-out, purposeful life mission statement, the following thought might be appropriate to consider: "If you don't know where you're going, any road will take you there and it doesn't matter how long it takes."

If you are looking for a mission worth all of vour time and effort, let me suggest two excellent sources as examples. The first is the Lord Jesus, who summarized His life and mission on earth this way: *"I glorified You on the earth, having accomplished the work which You have given Me to do"* (John 17.4). Whatever else we may pursue, the mission of every believer on earth is to lift up the name of Jesus, win His "Well done, good and faithful servant," and bring glory to God the Father by our lives.

The second example is Paul. For this I point to the passage from Philippians 3 that I quoted above. Paul had his "eyes on the prize" of serving and pleasing the Lord, and he let nothing deter him.

Lifelong growth and learning are so crucial because we are always the sum total of what we are becoming. This makes our aging years critically important because God's desire is that we keep growing and learning about who we are and where we are going. Aging provides the opportunity to live out what we are learning and becoming.

Having a mission statement is a crucial part of making sure you are going and growing in the right directions. These summary questions might help you to write a mission statement for your life now:

- What am I learning and how am I growing in these years?
- Who am I becoming?
- With all that I've had, in light of how I am growing now, and in light of my unique, God-given design, what do I believe is my "highest and best" contribution in advancing the cause of Christ on earth?
- Given my gifts and abilities, what type of activity offers the greatest potential for service to the Lord and others?
- In what direction is God leading me to invest my time, talent, and treasure?
- What are the opportunities in my life now?

Perhaps sharing my mission statement for this season of my life may help give you some ideas. As a believer in my 70s, I am trusting God to use my gifts of encouragement and teaching:

- to equip and motivate retiring boomers and those beyond in the prime of their lives
- to deepen their love for Jesus, and
- to use the talents and gifts God has given them to make their best contributions throughout the remaining years of their lives.

As you formulate your mission statement, don't forget to take into account your church and its ministries to its senior members and attenders. What kinds of activities are taking place in your church to encourage you and other seniors to make these years the best growing years of life? How can you contribute your gifts, skills, and commitments to enhance the ministry of your church to its seniors—and all ages, for that matter?

We've considered the importance and the benefits of continuing to grow in our aging years. Now let's talk about some of the barriers to growth that life and the enemy of our souls, Satan, often throw in our path to trip us up and knock us out of the race.

I've gleaned some great insights from the people in our *Seven Essentials* sessions as I've taught this series in churches and other venues around the country. Here are some of the things we identified that can keep us from growing:

- Fear
- Sin
- Power of Satan (he doesn't want us to grow!)
- Lack of self-confidence
- Isolation
- Casualness
- Busyness
- Lack of courage
- No sense of mission, lack of direction or goals

Consider the words of James in response to the barriers in life that keep us from growing. His exhortation can make a difference in how we view our hardships as we age:

> *Consider it all joy, my brethren, when you encounter various trials, knowing that the testing of your faith produces endurance. And let endurance have its perfect result, so that you may be perfect and complete, lacking in nothing. But if any of you lacks wisdom, let him ask of God, who gives to all generously and without reproach, and it will be given to him.* James 1.2–5

Yes, growing may seem harder as we age because growth means change. I believe our natural resistance to change is one reason for the well-known image of older men in particular as "grumpy old men." This has been the theme of countless jokes and even several movies, and the reason it resonates with people is that there is a lot of truth to it.

My friend Randy Hess, my co-host on our FWM podcasts, said he thinks this grumpiness comes when an older man no longer sees any meaning or purpose to life:

> *As you retire, the message you hear is to just get around, enjoy yourself, watch TV, play cards or play golf, if you can still do that. If you can't get around, then just sit back in your chair. Occasionally have a grandchild or someone else come and say hello, and that's all you need. But then you start getting grumpy because your life is meaningless, sitting there thinking about maybe an ailment you have, or what you no longer are able to do.*
>
> *My hunch is that if you are starting to feel that grumpiness, it's a message from the Lord saying to you, 'Wake up, you're still able to grow and influence other people, to make a difference in their lives.' As aging men we have wisdom we've gained, so in this part of our lives called the fourth quarter, we can begin to use that for good.* Randy Hess

That's a good word. We mentioned earlier the goal of Satan to keep us as believers from growing into all that God has for us. Satan is truly our enemy who seeks to destroy us (1 Peter 5.8). His mission is to *"steal and kill and destroy"* (John 10.10). Paul reminds us that we are constantly engaged in a spiritual war with our enemy. But we have the armor of God for our defense and victory. All we have to do is put it on every day, as Paul described:

> *Finally, be strong in the Lord and in the strength of His might. Put on the full armor of God, so that*

you will be able to stand firm against the schemes of the devil. For our struggle is not against flesh and blood, but against the rulers, against the powers, against the world forces of this darkness, against the spiritual forces of wickedness in the heavenly places. Therefore, take up the full armor of God, so that you will be able to resist in the evil day, and having done everything, to stand firm.
Ephesians 6.10–13

A Final Word

I want to end this chapter on a positive note. When I think about my mission in life, I appreciate the words of Pulitzer Prize-winning author Frederick Buechner on vocation:

"Vocation comes from the Latin *vocare*, "to call," and means the work a person is called to by God. There are all different kinds of voices calling you to all different kinds of work, and the problem is to find out which is the voice of God rather than of society, say, or the superego, or self-interest.

"By and large a good rule for finding out is this: The kind of work God usually calls you to is the kind of work (a) that you need to do and (b) that the world needs to have done. If you really get a kick out of your work, you've presumably met requirement (a), but if your work is writing cigarette ads, the chances are you've missed requirement (b). On the other hand, if your work is being a doctor in a leper colony, you have probably met requirement (b), but if most of the time you're bored and depressed by it, the chances are you have not only bypassed (a), but probably aren't helping your patients much either.

"Neither the hair shirt nor the soft berth will do. The place God calls you to is the place where your deep gladness and the world's deep hunger meet." (Originally published in *Wishful Thinking* and later in *Beyond Words*.)

And to further sharpen your thinking and motivation for growth, consider these selected quotes:

"I am 72, and I have determined at that I will keep learning every year for the rest of my life. I never want to stop learning." President George W. Bush

"Anyone who stops learning is old, whether at twenty or eighty. Anyone who keeps learning stays young." Henry Ford

"The future belongs to the learning, not to the learned." Mary Louise Rowand, former board member, American Bible Society

"In times of change learners inherit the earth; while the learned find themselves beautifully equipped to deal with a world that no longer exists." Eric Hoffer

"Once you stop learning, you start dying." Albert Einstein

"When you stop studying, you are dead." Lewis Sperry Chafer, late Founder and President, Dallas Theological Seminary

"When your memories are more exciting than your dreams, you've begun to die." Dr. Howard G. Hendricks

"You never get old until your regrets take the place of your dreams." Bill Gaither, Gaither Music

"A man does not grow old, but one becomes old by not growing." Fred Smith

CHAPTER TWO

The Second Essential:
The Importance of Connecting

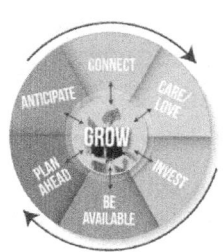

As this cartoon illustrates, connecting with others does not happen automatically, but takes deliberate effort and commitment.

Another way to illustrate this is by the experience of a long-time pastor in the Dallas area. A woman who attended his church came to him one day very upset and said, "I was in the hospital for a week, and no one from the church came to visit me, or even called to see how I was! No one cared!"

This wise pastor, who had had experiences like this before, asked the woman if she had called the church to let them know she was ill. The answer was no; apparently, she expected him just to know that.

Then the pastor asked her if she was a member of a Sunday school class, or one of the church's Bible study groups for women. Again, the answer was no. The pastor then said to her, "Well, the reason no one came or called is because no one knew about your illness." In other words, this woman had not established any connections with people in the church who could have reached out to her in her time of need.

That's a great illustration of the importance of the second essential for aging well. This woman liked attending the church, but she was content to do so in isolation—until she had a crisis. Then she wanted to be surrounded by caring people. She wanted connections.

When I talk about the importance of connecting, I mean the value of relationships and friendships that help us grow wherever we are in life. As we've seen, God has a plan for us to grow throughout our lives; now I want to consider with you the fact that this plan involves other people. I love this African proverb: "If you want to go fast, go alone. If you want to go far, go together." That's really wise. It takes strong relationships to keep growing.

Isolation and Aging

That's why living in isolation—failing to establish vital relationships with others—is so debilitating as we age. It's not the way God intends us to live. We are wired for relationships. God has built this principle into all of His creation. Even an atom does not exist by itself. Not only do atoms come together to form everything we see, but even an individual atom exists in a relationship of nucleus, protons, and electrons.

I'm also reminded of the importance of relationships whenever I see migrating geese in flight. Where I grew up, I watched the geese go back and forth on their migration during the various seasons. As we know, they all fly together and help each other if one falls. They draft off of the leader in their formation, and they change leaders as one tires.

But one problem many aging people face is isolation, being and/or feeling alone. It may seem that isolation is inevitable as we grow older; it just comes with the territory, so to speak. It can often creep in, rather than hitting us all at once. That can make it harder to detect, so that by the time we realize what's happening we find ourselves isolated from others.

One challenge we face is that aging is by its nature an isolating process. It can take away our career, the places where we spent maybe forty years or more building relationships and working with others. Aging can also take away our health, mobility—perhaps even our car. When we were working and raising our families, our homes were spinning with life and activity. But now we don't move as fast as we used to, and we don't get out as much.

In a society that prioritizes and even worships youth, we may also feel that no one pays attention to us anymore, or that nobody is interested in what we have to say. Last, but certainly not least, there are also the human losses of family members, friends, or even a spouse.

Added to that is the possible loss of regular contact with other family members. Our children are busy with their lives and families, and maybe they don't call or visit as often as they used to. The grandkids are busy too, and especially if they live in another place, we may not see or hear from them very often.

That's quite a list! You can see why some older people simply give up, retreat into their recliner or rocking chair, and let life pass them by. This can also lead to the bitterness of wondering why nobody calls, writes, visits, texts, or whatever anymore—expecting others to do all the work of staying in touch and building relationships while we sit, nurse our ailments and complaints, and become focused on ourselves, much like the woman in the opening example.

It's true that no one is exempt from the struggles of aging. But that doesn't mean we are doomed to live isolated lives. That's not the kind of life I want to live in the last two or three decades of my life, and I believe you don't want that either. It's become something of a mantra at FWM: We will not live alone; we will continue to build strong friendships, both for our benefit and enrichment and that of others.

The Incredible Value of Connecting

If one picture is worth a thousand words, we can learn a lot from this photo of a bicycle race, and even more from the accompanying graph.

I mentioned earlier that I'm a cyclist. I love cycling. This picture is a bicycle peloton, a group of riders who stay together during a race because it helps them. Now look at the graph, which really opens our eyes to the value of relationships. The rider in front must expend 86 percent of his energy to maintain the lead because of the wind coming at him and the crosswinds. The riders on the edges also expend more energy because they're absorbing the pounding of the crosswinds.

But the riders in the middle and back of the peloton only need to expend a small fraction of their energy to maintain the same pace because they are drafting off the riders in front of and around them. The riders in the back are only expending 5 percent of their energy to ride at the same speed as the leader. It's really an amazing phenomenon, and a great picture of the value of relationships.

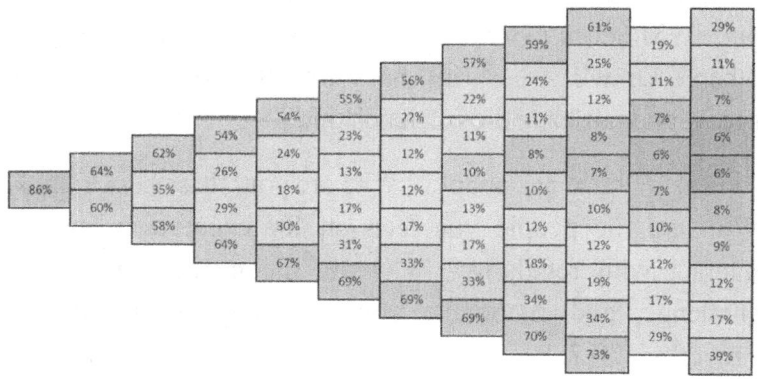

God's Word has a lot to say about the value of friendships, so let me give you some biblical foundations for this issue. Ecclesiastes 4.9–12 says:

Two are better than one because they have a good return for their labor. For if either of them falls, the one will lift up his companion. But woe to the one who falls when there is not another to lift him up. Furthermore, if two lie down together they keep warm, but how can one be warm alone? And if one can overpower him who is alone, two can resist him. A cord of three strands is not quickly torn apart.

These verses speak powerfully to the great benefit of friendships that bring warmth and comfort both to us and to the people we're connected with. I think this requires reaching out, taking the initiative to engage in continuing and growing friendships, and refusing to live isolated lives.

So, the questions I ask myself and the people who attend our FWM *Seven Essentials* conferences are, "Will we engage others? Or will we shrink back into the woodwork, so to speak, and not have those friendships?"

I also like to ask people, "Who are your three best friends? Who are the people you lean on for encouragement and interact with regularity? Who are the people who spark, challenge, and encourage you?" I love the imagery of Proverbs 27.17: *"Iron sharpens iron, so one man sharpens another."*

We all need sharpening now and then because we tend to become dull on our edges, like an axe that is used again and again but never sharpened. It's great to have a friend or family member who can sharpen us and allows us to do some sharpening too. I love getting together with people who know more than I do, just to listen, ask questions, offer my thoughts, and absorb their wisdom. The first thing I say when I meet someone is, "Tell me your story."

That's fun but consider this too. Sharpening iron on iron creates heat and friction that can produce sparks. In other words, this process can be painful at times. I never realized how selfish I was until I got married. But I discovered that doing life with another person in such an intimate way can spark friction. My wife Vicki doesn't think the way I think, and am I ever grateful for that! But still, relationships can cause friction, especially if someone needs to hear the truth.

As they say, the truth hurts. But if the person speaking the truth is a caring friend or loving spouse who you know has your best interests at heart, the truth may hurt but then heal. We just don't like to be corrected or even rebuked if necessary.

That's why it takes a true friend to risk it so that we can be better informed and *grow*. Having relationships makes such a huge difference in life. They can keep us from becoming set in our ways—grumpy old people who stick to our opinions and prejudices no matter what the truth is. Since I don't want to become like this, I surround myself with people who know they have my permission to challenge and stimulate me. I urge you to form those friendships too.

The Blessing of Christ's Body

Believers in Jesus Christ have a huge advantage here, because we have been formed into one unified spiritual body by the Holy Spirit. The apostle Paul explains: *"For even as the [human] body is one and yet has many members, and all the members of the body, though they are many, are one body, so also is [the body of] Christ"* (1 Corinthians 12.12).

If you are a follower of Christ, you have a vital connection with other Christians—which is one factor that makes church so important in connecting. This is why the Bible calls us brothers and sisters in Christ. No Christian needs to live in isolation when he or she is a member of the body of Christ. Read on in 1 Corinthians 12 and you'll see that each member is also vital to the proper functioning of Christ's body because we all have different roles to play.

This is another powerful reason for you and me to be connected. Your gifts and skills are uniquely needed; but if you isolate yourself, you're depriving the body of your giftedness as a part the body needs to function the way God intended. And you're also depriving yourself of the giftedness and ministry of others to you so that you function the way God intended.

Now, after decades in church ministry, I know better than most that churches aren't perfect, because the people in them aren't perfect. You may have visited a church and not felt welcome, or tried to reach out and were rejected. But that doesn't mean you quit and go home. You've probably had more than one bad meal at a restaurant, but you haven't stopped eating.

God places such a high value on relationships that the writer of Hebrews tells us: *"And let us consider how to stimulate one another to love and good deeds, not forsaking our own assembling together, as is the habit of some, but encouraging **one another**; and all the more as you see the day drawing near"* (Hebrews 10.24–25).

The word "stimulate" is a strong one. The old *King James Version* used the word "provoke," which usually has a negative connotation. But the idea here is to not provoke each other in the wrong way, but to strongly encourage and urge each other to get and stay connected. So, as we age the relationships we form are absolutely critical, for one reason to help us resist the isolation that creeps in, so we grow and become the men, women, seniors, and elders that God calls us to be.

Allow me to play "cheerleader" for a moment and make a strong appeal for the incredible importance of connecting with others. The apostle Paul said in looking over his life: *"I do not regard myself as having laid hold of it yet; but one thing I do: forgetting what lies behind and reaching forward to what lies ahead, **I press on** toward the goal for the prize of the upward call of God in Christ Jesus"* (Philippians 3.13–14).

My friend, I urge you as I do myself, let's "press on" as we age! There are lives and families at stake, loved ones and friends who need what you have to offer. Consider these crucial reasons that God has called us to connect with others in our older years:

- To pour into the lives of the generations following us, to mentor younger people around us
- To continue strengthening friendships in this mission—to "carry the flag" in our churches and our communities, encouraging our peers to finish well
- To pray for our families—our grown kids, grandkids, and great grandkids

You are on the way to finishing well when you position yourself mentally and spiritually to say, "I feel like there's more I can contribute, and I'm ready to help somebody." Whether that somebody is a family member, friend, or even somebody you've met casually at church or wherever, think about how you can reach out and try to make a difference for that person.

Don't misunderstand me. This is not poking your nose in other people's lives and offering them something they don't need. Pray for discernment and grace and be willing to connect. I've taught FWM seminars in enough senior living centers, churches, and other places to know that there is always someone God has put in my life who needs encouragement, guidance, or just a listening ear.

What about that person in your life with whom you've had negative experiences, or just feel distanced from for some reason? Remember we said that connecting with others won't always be easy. A lot of people would just write that person off and move on. There may be any number of reasons for the disconnect, but God may not want you to cut off that relationship because this person may be the very one who needs you the most. However, his or her guard is up for some reason—perhaps to guard against another hurt or rejection. Part of showing grace is trying to get beyond those feelings and finding out what that person needs.

What we're talking about is a decision to age in a way that removes us from ourselves and our hurts and restrictions so that we can help the people we care about, those who need us. Begin thinking like that, and you'll never lack for someone to connect with. As I grow, I'm learning and being reminded every day that life is not all about me, but about what I can do to impact other people in positive ways.

The Challenges of Connecting

Connecting with other people in meaningful ways is a challenge for everybody. Not only do we have the limitations that come with aging, but we have different personalities. Some people are just naturally more outgoing, while others are more reticent.

Personality plays a definite role in this. Sometimes people look at guys like me and say, "It's probably easy for you to connect with people, Hal. You were a pastor for all those years, and you've been teaching and working with people for years. You obviously enjoy meeting and relating to people because you're an extrovert. I'm just not like that."

It's true that I'm more of an outgoing person. I engage people all the time. So, I readily acknowledge that intentionally connecting with people can be harder for more introverted people. If you're in that category, let me encourage you to take a step of faith and reach out. Perhaps you could begin by praying for opportunities to engage another person if you don't have those now. When God opens a door like that with someone else, you'll know it.

And remember, you don't have to be a highly polished conversationalist or an expert on everything to engage someone in a meaningful connection. As I said earlier, I like to ask questions that help me get to know the other person—and let's face it, we all like to talk about ourselves. You may even want to start with a phone call or a card . . . a lost art, I know.

By the way, here's a great tip on connecting, and it's free. Sending a card with a short note is something most older people have time to do. I have a friend whose wife sends out so many cards to people they know and love, young and old, on every occasion possible that their post office keeps running out of stamps. The responses over the years have been phenomenal—from tears to calls to emails to hugs in church, all saying how much the card meant.

This person is not using cards as a substitute for face-to-face communication, but as a supplement to it. You'll be amazed at how your relationship with someone will be transformed if he or she has just received a card from you expressing your love, prayers, congratulations, sympathy, etc. But be careful; you might get a hug!

So even if you're an extreme introvert, you still need other people, and they need you. Maybe you can't do a card. What about an email or text, if you do those sorts of things? Or a phone call. I think what stops us a lot of times is thinking that this person doesn't really want to hear from me or need what I have to offer, so I'm just wasting my time doing all of this. But so often this simply is not true.

The Enemy of Connecting

I have discovered over the years that these kinds of isolating, discouraging, self-defeating thoughts are often the work of Satan, the enemy of our souls. That shouldn't surprise, because we know from Scripture that Satan has access to our minds to plant doubts, temptations, and all kinds of discouraging thoughts to weaken us and render us ineffective for Christ.

And I'm convinced that one of the devil's great schemes is to keep us isolated from one another, trying to convince us that we really don't have anything to contribute to others; that people don't need or want us; that since we may have been hurt by others in the past, reaching out is not worth the risk; that others should take the initiative to reach out to us; etc., etc.

Can you see how believing these things can drive us into hiding, into ourselves? When I become completely self-absorbed, I'm not much good to anyone, including myself. But here's the good news about Satan's attempts to bring us down. The Bible reveals his battle plan, and how we can defeat it!

Paul told the Corinthians that "*we are not ignorant of his [the devil's] schemes*" (2 Corinthians 2.11). "Schemes" here means "plans, plots." We can resist and defeat Satan through the Word of God and prayer, and when we stand firm, we have this promise: "*Resist the devil and he will flee from you*" (James 4,7; read about Jesus' temptation in Matthew 4.11).

Building Lasting Friendships

So rather than withdrawing and hiding, I choose to connect with others and form lasting friendships. The benefits are incredibly enriching. I think of this when I read, "*A friend loves at all times, and a brother is born for adversity*" (Proverbs 17.17). You go through life with friends with whom you laugh, celebrate milestones, and so forth.

But there are also special friends who God places in your life to lift you up and help you grow through the difficult times. I call them friends for life. If you have one or more of these in your life, they are God's gift. You can talk about anything with them and know it is safe, especially those things you don't care to share with the world.

We saw a great illustration of this when my wife Vicki had her second foot surgery. Lifelong friends came to our house one evening, and we visited for three hours. It was a fascinating time reviewing the four-plus decades of our friendship—talking about issues, things we've experienced and struggle with even today. We finished our conversation by going around the table and asking, "What can I pray about for you?" The four of us shared things from our lives that we wanted each other to pray for.

The question of friendship is, how willing am I to share what's on my heart and pray for my friends so we all can continue growing together? Jesus did that with His disciples. In the Upper Room the night before His crucifixion, Jesus said to them: "*I have called you friends, for all things that I have heard from My Father I have made known to you*" (John 15.15). That's a very remarkable statement. The eternal Son of God opened His heart and life to the men who had spent three-and-a-half years with Him. Jesus wanted and needed close friends around Him—and His circle of friendship was not limited to the apostles. John 15.15 is also spoken to every child of God.

I think of Jesus' example as a standard for friendships in this season of life. In the last two or three decades following retirement, we face the challenges of adjusting to a new routine and a new mission, along with aging and all the issues that go with it. How easily do we share those things with our friends? And how often do we work through them together and encourage each other?

Think about it. Even the Son of God did not want be alone and isolated while He was on earth! I'm intrigued by the reasons Jesus chose His twelve disciples to spend His ministry with. Yes, it was to accomplish the mission of spreading the gospel and building the church.

But notice also what this verse says about Jesus choosing the Twelve: "*And He appointed twelve, **so that they would be with Him** and that he could send them out to preach*" (Mark

3.14). Jesus invested His life in relationships, and He does that with each of His disciples, as I said above.

No wonder the thrust of God's Word to the church is for us to be vitally connected with each other in life-giving, life-building relationships. We used to hear it said that God never intended for us to be Lone Ranger Christians. Here's the writer of Hebrews encouraging the church (a text we quoted above). But look at the all the plural pronouns:

> *Therefore, since **we** have so great a cloud of witnesses surrounding **us**, let **us** also lay aside every encumbrance and the sin which so easily entangles **us**, and let **us** run with endurance the race that is set before **us**, fixing **our** eyes on Jesus, the author and perfecter of faith, who for the joy set before Him endured the cross, despising the shame, and has sat down at the right hand of the throne of God.* Hebrews 12.1–2

We are meant to be a "convoy" heading down the road of life in close connection with others. This is the terms that gerontologists Antonucci and Akiyama use to describe the importance of connectedness in the aging years. It's a bit of a long read, but worth reflecting on:

> *The Convoy Model of Social Relations calls for radical friendship in every community.* **The term convoy is used to evoke the image of a protective layer, in this case, of family, friends, & colleagues who surround us and help us to negotiate life's many challenges and opportunities.** *Each of us, if we are fortunate, are moving through life*

surrounded and supported by a group of people with whom we receive and give support. I think our convoys are dynamic and, if we are fortunate, lifelong in nature, changing in some ways but remaining stable in other ways across time and situations. I have a rich convoy or a band of brothers and sisters, consisting of family, trusted old friends from childhood, fraternity brothers, military friends, academic colleagues, students, and even Narnia-like creatures." (Taken from "The Social Networks in Adult Life and a Preliminary Examination of the Convoy Model, (Toni C. Antonucci, Hiroko Akiyama *Journal of Gerontology*, Volume 42, Issue 5, September 1987, pp. 519–527).

Several More Thoughts

The scourge of COVID-19 taught all of us some painful lessons about the importance of connecting with the people in our lives. We were cut off for months, and the results were devastating for many. Even now, a lot of churches and other organizations are still building back their congregations and audiences.

For the first time in most of our lives, the prospect of getting together with other people was fraught with fear, and larger gatherings were often banned. Many people were forced to work at home, and so they lost the face-to-face interaction with their colleagues. COVID became a new barrier to connecting that we didn't have any control over. I'm hearing of people who still won't go out to church or anywhere in public, even with a mask in some cases.

The pandemic barrier is slowly resolving itself, and we've talked about other barriers that keep us from connecting. Here are some barriers we discussed in our group sessions. I repeat them here to help you identify the barrier or barriers that you may need to work on:

- The risk of rejections and pain of past rejections
- Our culture may not value older folks
- Physical limitations
- Our failures
- Past hurts, feeling that people may not want to connect with you
- Our sense of worth, feeling as if we have little or nothing to offer

And then for your encouragement, and as idea starters, here are some of the ways we brainstormed on how to connect and form relationships with others:

I want to end this chapter with a wonderful statement that summarizes so well all that we've been saying about the importance of connecting with other people:

> *You and I are hardwired for relationships. We were created by God to love and to be loved by others. We were created for much more than casual friendships or acquaintances. We need deep and meaningful relationships with those God has put*

into our lives. *We need people who will walk with us through the ups and downs of life, who will be there for us when times get tough, and who will look to us for help and support in their own struggles.*

"*We need people who will intentionally invest in our lives. People who will pray for us when we are sick, counsel us when we're confused, laugh with us when we are happy, defend us when we're under fire, and offer a shoulder to cry on when life gets hard and cumbersome. People who will always be there for us, no matter what. People who need us as much as much as we need them.* Jim Stump, The Power of One-On-One: Discovering the Joy and Satisfaction of Mentoring Others, p.141

This is our mission. Please join with me in fulfilling it!

CHAPTER THREE

The Third Essential:
The Importance of Caring/Loving

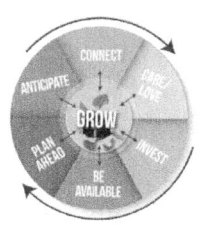

In this *Third Essential for Finishing Well*, we'll discuss how important it is to love and care for each other—to be there for others in their needs. I believe we can do this because I see aging saints as a convoy, a peloton (per the diagram in chapter 2) of strength for Christ and for future generations. The apostle Paul said: "*I can do all things through Him [Christ] who strengthens me*" (Philippians 4.13).

With this promise of Christ's strength for us in mind, our model throughout this chapter will be Him, our Lord Jesus Christ, both in His incredible, never-ending love for us, and in His command to us to love others as He loves us.

The Depth of Jesus' Love for Us

Let's look at His life first and reflect on the depth of His love and care for us. In the Upper Room with His disciples, the night before His crucifixion, Jesus said: "*A new commandment I give to you, that you love one another, **even as I have loved you**, that you also love one another*" (John 13.34).

That's much deeper than loving your neighbor as yourself, although Jesus commanded us to do that also (Matthew 22.39). This is loving others the way Jesus loves us, which was all the way to the cross. And then Jesus said, *"By this all men will know that you are my disciples, if you have love for one another"* (John 13.35). Having "Jesus-love" for others puts things in a new light that we don't often think about in relating with others.

In the same Upper Room discourse, Jesus told His disciples that He was sending the Holy Spirit, who would *"teach you all things, and bring to your remembrance all that I said to you"* (John 14.26). We have the Holy Spirit within us as believers, so as I go through life the Spirit is leading my mind, heart, emotions, and sensitivities to put me in a position to meet other people's needs. This includes everyone from my family and friends to the people around me in church, and wherever I go.

So, in a very real sense, loving and caring for others is not simply something I do when it's convenient or when I feel like it. It's actually a matter of obeying the Holy Spirit and responding as Jesus would. This is not just performance; Jesus has set me free to give my life away, just as He freely gave His life away.

This is clear from Paul's prayer in Philippians 1.9: *"And this I pray, that your love may abound still more and more in real knowledge and all discernment."* After stating his confidence that God would complete the work of salvation that He had begun in the Philippians believers, Paul urged them to "overflow" in their love both for Christ and for each other. It's because Jesus loved us first that we can love and care as He does.

To fulfill this essential for aging well (Jesus' command, actually) to love others as He loves us means we must pay attention to the people around us. I realize this can be hard for some older people to get their minds around because they are already dealing with the issues and struggles that often come with their own aging. I'm not suggesting that you neglect yourself to care for others. I have a friend who says you have to be a missionary to yourself before you can be a missionary to others.

However, I am saying that in order to love and care for people the way I'm talking about requires that we tune into a different wavelength that we may not otherwise be sensitive to. And I want you to see two very important truths as we progress through this chapter:

> **First,** we are so secure in Jesus' unfailing love for us that we can confidently reach out and care for others in His strength with no fear that Jesus' love for us will be diminished at all. His love gives us a solid foundation on which to stand.
>
> **Second,** no matter what the limitations of our aging years, Jesus can and will make us adequate for any assignment He gives us.

I highlighted these truths because you must get them fixed in your mind and believe them with all your heart before you can be effective in loving and caring for others. And just to cement them in your mind more clearly, let's briefly review the nature and extent of Jesus' love for us.

The Ways Jesus Loves Us

One of the most amazing prophecies in all of Scripture speaks to the intense suffering Jesus endured for us during His trials, when He was beaten mercilessly, and on the cross. The prophet Isaiah wrote:

> *Surely our griefs He Himself bore, and our sorrows He carried; yet we ourselves esteemed Him stricken, smitten of God, and afflicted. But He was pierced through for our transgressions, He was crushed for our iniquities; the chastening for our well-being fell upon Him, and by His scourging we are healed. All of us like sheep have gone astray, each of us has turned to His own way; but the* LORD *has caused the iniquity of us all to fall on Him.* Isaiah 53.4–6

Jesus endured unimaginable suffering to pay for our sins so we could be forgiven and have eternal life. Having considered all that Jesus has done for us, it should be our joy to share His love and care with those in need around us. I use the word "joy" deliberately because of the statement we've seen before in Hebrews 12:2 that Jesus endured the cross because of *"the joy set before him."*

The joy for Jesus in spite of the cross was that of knowing that He was providing our salvation. His is the supreme example of the love and care that He has commanded us to show to others. We can't do it perfectly as Jesus did, but our relationships can be marked by His self-sacrificing love. Just as Jesus was not casually connected to us, but loved us in deep and profound ways, so we are called to love others. Let's explore how we can do that in these aging years—which can be our best years!

Loving and Caring Like Jesus

The apostle Paul knew what it meant to love like Jesus, and Paul also knew what it would take to do this effectively. He wrote:

> *Have this attitude in yourselves which was also in Christ Jesus, who, although He existed in the form of God, did not regard equality with God a thing to be grasped, but emptied Himself, taking the form of a bond-servant, and being made in the likeness of men. Being found in appearance as a man, He humbled Himself by becoming obedient to the point of death, even death on a cross.*
> Philippians 2.5–8

I try to remind myself every day how much Jesus loves me. He laid down His life for me! And today, He pays attention to my needs and answers my prayers. He is absorbed with His love for me, without any conditions. Regardless of what other people around me do, I'm deeply focused and thrilled with the attention that God has for me. If I lose this, I have no real capacity to love others because I'm consumed with my own issues. There's a big difference between being self-absorbed and being confident that, because I know how much Jesus loves me and is looking out for my needs, I have a platform to engage with other people to help meet their needs. That platform must be built on the truth of Jesus' love for me.

We could summarize Jesus' life as the One who gave eternal encouragement to everyone He met. I may not have the means to meet certain needs that people have, but I can always encourage them. So, I ask myself constantly, how much do I encourage my wife, my adult children, my grandchildren? How much do I say, "I love you; I appreciate you, you make a difference in my life"? To give true encouragement to others, we need to be invested in their lives, to know what they're going through and how we can help them. Jesus didn't just throw out random words of encouragement. He knew people—where they were hurting and how they needed to be uplifted.

Jesus' life of love and service is our example, and He has called us to serve and love as He did. In the Upper Room, on the night before His crucifixion, Jesus humbled Himself by washing His disciples' feet. Then He told them, *"Do you know what I have done to you? You call Me Teacher and Lord; and you are right, for **so** I am. If I then, the Lord and the Teacher, washed your feet, you also ought to wash one another's feet"* (John 13.12–14). We're to serve others with our lives. We're not exempt from this command just because we're a little bit older.

Sensing and Meeting People's Needs

The way we learn to love like Jesus is by being alert to sense and meet the needs of those around us. This may be anything from a word of encouragement and prayer to doing something tangible to help meet a need. Doing this requires time, a listening ear, and a compassionate heart—all the traits Jesus displayed during His ministry on earth. He spent time with people, listened to their concerns and hurts, and then touched and healed them.

We are certainly not healers as Jesus was, but our words and actions can have a healing effect on others in many ways. This requires something of us, for sure; our time, for example. We're not all equal in material resources, but we all have the same number of hours in a day. We use the term "spending" time with someone because loving and caring will cost us the investment of time—something many of us actually have more of in our aging years than we did when we were busy carving out a career and raising children. And yet, my experience is that many people are more reluctant to spend their time than they are even their money.

That's why so many people are glad to donate money, clothes, or food to a local charity—but going out to deliver those goods and meet a poor family, maybe getting involved with them, is another story. Many Christians are glad to put a check in the offering plate to help reach lost people for Christ—but taking the time to go out and engage people as a personal witness for Christ is another story. "I don't want to get involved" has become a mantra in America.

Don't get me wrong. Our gifts and donations are always desperately needed. But I'm talking about loving and caring for others in person, investing our lives in the people we care about most and those whom God puts in our path. This follows inevitably when we make the connections that I talked about in the *Second Essential* for finishing well. The COVID shutdown taught us the value of relationships in an unforgettable way as people were literally cut off from others. We are still recovering from this as a society.

In my case, connecting and cultivating relationships begins at home with my wife, Vicki. I know what many of her needs are because I have spent so much time with her. But it's not an automatic process. I still need to listen to her and ask the right questions, because her needs and desires are different at different times. The same is true with my grown children and grandchildren, and the people in my church, Sunday school class, the life group I teach, and those in my ministry network, neighborhood, and larger community.

We can't do everything, but we can give a listening ear and time, even if all we have to give is a few minutes and not hours. I'm sure you have experienced, as I have, that ten minutes with a caring friend can be the most impactful thing that happens to us in any given day, week, or even month. The great thing about this is that you don't need a degree in psychology to love and care for others. In many cases, all you have to do is pay attention to what they're saying and try to sense the need behind the words. I often ask myself: Do I listen? Do I follow up with a phone call or a card? Simple things like this can start us on a wonderful road of caring for each other. A well-known pastor once said, "Preach to broken hearts and you will never lack for an audience."

That's true, which is why I want to begin my day by asking God to lead me to people whose needs I can meet. And before we go any farther, let me emphasize again that these don't have to be huge, life-altering needs, or something tragic. It could be a pat on the back and a "Well done!" But the point of this essential of loving and caring means that we don't say to someone, "I love you," and then go our way without doing anything for them. The apostle James cautioned us about saying empty words that have no impact:

> *"If a brother or sister is without clothing and in need of daily food, and one of you says to them, 'Go in peace, be warmed and be filled,' and yet you do not give them what is necessary for **their** body, what use is that?"* (James 2.15–16).

And it in case it's not clear by now, this is not a one-way street. I've been doing ministry for a long time, and I have never met anyone who told me, "Hal, I've spent years caring for and loving others, and no one has ever asked me about my needs or how I'm doing." I don't think such a person exists! The old adage, "To have a friend, be a friend" still has a lot of truth to it. As we impact other people's lives, they also pour into our lives.

Caring for and loving others is a two-way street; my emphasis in this essential for finishing well is on what I can do at my end of the street. Vicki is really good at encouraging others. She will think of someone she hasn't heard from for too long, and make a phone call, if possible, to see how that person is. One Mother's Day, she sat at a table on our patio and made a series of phone calls to women who have really poured their lives into her. Each call was about 15-20 minutes, just to thank these women for their impact in her life. I've gotten feedback from people I've contacted who say, "That meant more to me than you could ever imagine."

Another great thing about this ministry of caring and loving is that it can cross generations. Vicki and I were able to help a young couple who were devastated after their third miscarriage. We had that opportunity because we had been pouring our lives into theirs. We grieved with them and encouraged them with the reminder that God still has a purpose in their lives.

In Romans 8.29, the apostle Paul talks about the importance of being conformed to the image of Christ. This is what it means to grow and mature as a Christian. We may think that as people in the latter decades of life, we're already mature. But spiritual maturity is a lifelong process and goal, and I want to suggest that these latter decades of our lives might be the best years ever for maturing in Christ.

We have the breadth of our lives behind us to see what God has done, and now we can begin to see what He still wants to do with us in terms of the impact we can make with our lives. My commitment is to say, "I will care, I will love, I will be there for others in their needs. I will love others as Christ commands me to love." My challenge to you is, let's join together in living out this commitment.

The Focus of Our Lives

None of what we've looked at so far will be possible as long as we are self-focused. To someone like this, other people are a barrier; they get in the way of what this person thinks he or she needs to be happy. Self-absorbed people cut themselves off from caring, loving family and friends who could enrich their lives and help them experience true fulfillment. These are people who want what they want when they want it, and they usually don't care what it costs others to get it.

Jesus had a lot to say about the focus of our lives. In Matthew 6.33, He said: *"But seek first [God's] kingdom and His righteousness, and all these things will be added to you,"* that is, the things we need to sustain life and the extra blessings God has in store for us. Here's what even too many Christians don't understand. They're afraid that if they put God and others first in life, they'll somehow have to give up everything and lose out on all the good stuff. But Jesus said that when we put Him first, we gain everything that matters.

And because God's kingdom here on earth includes other people, my passion should be to serve Him and serve others. In fact, one of the best ways we can serve God is by caring for and loving the people He sent Jesus to die for. When we live with this passion and focus, we can understand why Paul said that we don't need to be anxious or worried about anything (Philippians 4.6).

So instead of asking who are the people and situations that are getting in the way of my self-fulfillment, I need to ask what things are getting in the way of my becoming more like

Jesus. Of course, there are physical, mental, and emotional obstacles we have to deal with as aging people, the aches and pains of everyday life. And the COVID pandemic has left a lot of older people living in fear, afraid to go out or reach out. I understand these things because I'm living them along with you. But I also hear the voice of Jesus saying, "I want you to love others as I have loved you." So, I feel the Holy Spirit leading me, encouraging me, nudging me on to be more like Christ during these important years.

A big part of that Christ-likeness I want to grow in is caring for and loving others just as Jesus continues to care for and love me. That's great to know, because I need His care and love more in my aging years than ever before. I get weary some days as I age, yet Jesus' love and care is steadfast, and He wants me to show love to others as well.

Some Final Thoughts

The people we spend the most time with can have a huge impact on our ability to care for and love others. A man once said, "I think we are the summation of our five best friends." There's a lot of wisdom in that, so let me ask you: Are the people you hang out with encouraging you to get beyond yourself and love others? If you have friends like this, you are rich. But if your friends are hindering your growth in Christ, you may need to cultivate some new friendships. I want friends who pull me out of myself when I start to become too self-focused and help me keep my eyes focused on Jesus.

You might say at this point, "But Hal, you don't know how tough my life is." That's true, I don't know; but I know that even when life got tough for Jesus, He didn't opt out. My mother, who died at the of 96, spent the last two years of her life greatly debilitated. She needed help getting out of bed, and couldn't do anything for herself, so she had to go to an assisted living facility.

She could have felt sorry for herself and given up. But because she had cultivated such an amazing life of connecting with and loving others, there was a constant parade of women of all ages, whose lives she had touched, coming to see her. They would come to encourage mom, and she would pray for them. Mom was encouraged, and they would leave encouraged and blessed themselves. So just because life is diminished at a certain point doesn't mean we can't love and care for others. There are just different ways of doing it. My mother had an endless prayer list. She prayed from her bed day in and day out.

I'm a church guy, so I think of all this in terms of the church—the one place on earth that God has formed to be His care center. Imagine what it would be like if the strongest segment of a church body were its older people? Imagine how we could encourage each other and help the young people as they struggle with parenting, marriage, work, and other issues. The apostle Paul used two wonderful images to describe the care and love he had poured into the believers at the church in Thessalonica, which he had founded.

Paul said that he and his fellow workers had dealt with these people as gently and lovingly "*as a nursing mother cares for her own children*" (1 Thessalonians 2.7). And just a few verses later he said they encouraged and exhorted the people "*as a father would his own children*" (v. 11). What a tremendous picture of everything this essential is all about!

Before we close out this study, I need to say what you may already be thinking. It's not always easy to care for others. It can be exhausting for older people, in fact. Just ask any grandparent after a weekend of babysitting the grandkids! There are people who suck the life out of us; in our church we used to call them oxygen thieves. But when I think of this, I think about how I must have drained the life out of the adults who invested their lives in me. And I am eternally grateful to them.

Here's the bottom line. Aging presents a whole new set of challenges for us. Paul knew this, but he also knew how to overcome these challenges: *"Therefore we do not lose heart; though our outer man is decaying, yet our inner man is being renewed day by day"* (2 Corinthians 4.16).

Loving/Caring means...

- Growing and building relationships
- Continuing the dialogue by listening, learning, and taking it farther
- Ensuring the well-being of others—being a shepherd to love and care or them
- Having alertness to needs and doing something about those needs
- Being active, constantly vigilant for needs we can help meet

Barriers to Caring...

- Not having a sense of the future, or realizing the difference we can make in the life of another person
- Not realizing that God values me or knowing the difference I can make in the lives of others
- Having biases and prejudices against others which will preclude caring
- Not wanting to take risks, being fearful of "What will they think? "Will I be rejected?"
- Protecting myself from being hurt
- Spiritual warfare – Satan doesn't want me to get involved. Caring may draw me deeper into the spiritual battlegrounds of those for whom I care. Satan will tempt me to "play it safe" and if that doesn't work, he will attack me.

"Take away love and our earth is a tomb." Robert Browning

"What the heart gives away is never gone; it is kept in the hearts of others." Robin St. John

CHAPTER FOUR

The Fourth Essential:
The Importance of Investing in Younger Generations

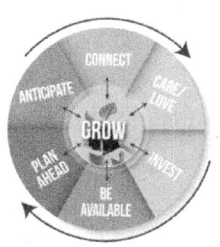

"The great use of life is to spend it for something that will outlast it." – William James

I hope we've established by now how easy it is for older people to lose sight of the purposes God has for them in their aging years. I'd like to suggest at least two of those purposes as we launch into the *Fourth Essential for Finishing Well*:

- First, God wants us to keep growing and trusting Him for all that He wants to be *to* us and *in* us. Regardless of the hardships we face, God wants us to keep growing, connecting, and caring for and loving those He puts in our lives (a summary of the first three essentials).
- Second, I'm convinced that God also desires and designs for us to invest our lives in the generations that follow us, beginning with our own families.

The Bible calls this discipleship, or disciple-making. The one command in Jesus' Great Commission is, "*Make disciples of all the nations*" (Matthew 28.19). By way of reminder, a disciple is a learner, or follower. This was the key to Jesus' ministry as He invested the majority of His time and energy in teaching the twelve men He had chosen, pouring His life into them.

For us, disciple-making involves pouring the life of Jesus through the Scriptures *and* our lives by way of example into the people God brings across our paths. If this sounds academic, it's not! The idea is that as an older person, I want to be so consumed with what God is doing in my life that I can't help but share His love and goodness with others. Biblical discipleship is carried out in daily life—and by the way, we can't beg off because we're older; this is Jesus' command to all of His people, because we are His disciples too!

The Bible on Investing

Investing in future generations is critical to having the right estimation of the value we hold as older people in our families, churches, and communities. The Bible has a lot to say about the value and crucial importance of building into the lives of those who are coming behind us. The psalmist David wrote:

> *O God, You have taught me from my youth, and I still declare Your wondrous deeds. And even when I am old and gray, O God, do not forsake me, until I declare Your strength to this generation,* **Your power to all who are to come.** Psalm 71.17–18

This is David's "old man" psalm. As he reflected on his life, David rejoiced in God's faithfulness to him, and he realized that the best thing he could do was to declare God's goodness to the generations coming behind him. That's a wonderful example for you and me, but I also know that sometimes as older people, we can feel as if the younger people don't want to hear what we must share. That can be very discouraging.

Let's face it. The aging process is often a time of alienation, of feeling alone and unnoticed. It's easy to feel distant from other people as we age and slow down. We've all known older people who wonder why God has left them here. They feel like their value is used up, and will say things like, "I don't want to be here anymore. I just want to go to heaven."

That's why I think David asked the Lord not to forsake him in his old age. This was stated as a prayer request, but it's really a statement of confidence because David knew God would be faithful to him until he had completed the assignment God had for his life—which included testifying of God's faithfulness to future generations.

You and I have this same assignment from God as part of our aging years. We are here to tell the story of God's faithfulness, abiding presence, and joy with others all around us, both with our contemporaries and, as we're emphasizing in this chapter, with those coming behind us. I tell people in our *Seven Essentials for Finishing Well* seminars that we're here to encourage each other, and to encourage our adult children and grandchildren who need this desperately in the world they are facing.

And even if we don't have children or grandchildren of our own, we need to look around us at church. There are younger people sitting around us every Sunday who need someone older to invest in their lives. We have the opportunity and responsibility to invest in them. Part of this investment is made by the testimony of our lives and words to others in the body of Christ.

You and I are witnessing to others even when we're not aware of it, because someone is always watching our lives, whether at church or in our homes, neighborhoods, and offices. We saw how deeply committed David was to ensuring that the generations coming behind him knew of God's goodness and faithfulness. Notice how this theme runs through other psalms:

> *So we, Your people and the sheep of Your pasture will give thanks to You forever; to all generations we will tell of Your praise.* Psalm 79.13
>
> *I will sing of the lovingkindness of the LORD forever; to all generations I will make known Your faithfulness with my mouth.* Psalm 89.1
>
> *One generation shall praise Your works to another and shall declare your mighty acts.* Psalm 145.3
>
> *For He established a testimony {a witness} in Jacob and appointed a law {a standard} in Israel, which He commanded our fathers that they should teach them **to their children, that the generation to come** might know, even **the children yet to be born**, that they may arise and tell them **to their children**, that they should put their **confidence in God** and not forget the works of God, but keep [obey] His commandments.* Psalm 78.5–7

Crawford Loritts, a wonderful Bible teacher and speaker, makes five vitally important observations growing out of this text in Psalm 78 (my emphasis):*

> 1. We need to be the **patriarchs and matriarchs** who will lead the way and call our families to trust God. God calls us to intentionally nurture and instill a "God-confidence" in the hearts of our grown kids and grandkids.
>
> 2. We are here to steward the vision of God from one generation to the next.
>
> 3. We will continue to teach our children, building on decade after decade, **telling the stories of God's faithfulness again and again.**
>
> 4. We will press **to fuel future generations** with a passion for the character of God and a confidence in the truth of Scripture.
>
> 5. As parents and grandparents, **we pray for the generations to come.** We pray for our grandkids and our great grandkids. **We pray for the generations that we will not see.**

*This is an incredible sermon preached at the first national conference of the Legacy Coalition. It's worth hearing. https://legacycoalition.com/63crawford-loritts-for-a-time-we-cannot-see/

These principles and the Psalms quoted above really drive home the truth that we, as older people, are to take the lead in this multi-generational discipling process. One reason I love these passages is that it's easy to forget that even though our children may be adults and have children of their own, they are still watching us to see how we respond to the pressures and challenges of life. And they're not just watching—they're also looking for clues as to how they should respond to their pressures and challenges. And we can be sure our grandchildren are paying attention to us, whether we think so or not.

That's why our example is so important, and why we need to make sure that no matter our age or limitations, we are growing in Christ and reflecting His life and wisdom to everyone around us. This is also why it is so very important that we tell our stories to the generations coming after us. Let your grandchildren know how you handled a situation, or how God was faithful to you in a particular circumstance. Your children may have seen these things firsthand when they were home, but they tend to forget what happened twenty or thirty years ago.

I have a friend who loves to remind his adult children of some incredible answers to prayer their family experienced when his children were preteens and early teens. He says they usually respond with a smile and sigh and say, "Yeah dad, we remember . . ." and then they finish the story. That means it's cemented in their minds and can still affect the way they think when they need to trust God for something that seems almost impossible, which is what this essential is all about.

Before we move on, I want to address an issue that is no doubt on many minds as we talk about multi-generational ministry; it may be on your mind as well. This is the issue of children or grandchildren who have walked away from the faith and are not living for the Lord. It's possible for good and godly parents to invest heavily in raising their children to love and serve the Lord, only to see them turn and make decisions that neither they nor God would want them to make. This can be a real heartbreaker, and there are no easy answers for it.

But there is something we can do about wayward kids. Along with the obvious ministry of continuing our witness to and prayers for them, we can ultimately trust God to honor the investment we've made in their lives, even if we don't live to see the return on that investment. That can be especially true with grandchildren. We know God is trustworthy and His Word is true, so we can cling to His promises as we continue to pour our lives and love into the generations behind us. We may not know the outcome, but we can trust God with the investment that He has made in us, and we in them. But this is not the situation we want, so let's talk about how to be a steward of a godly vision for those coming behind us.

Stewarding a Vision

We don't use the word "steward" much anymore, but a steward had great responsibility in Bible times. A steward was the manager or caretaker of the owner's property, and often oversaw the rearing and education of the boss's children. That's why the number one trait a steward needed was trustworthiness, as Paul explained: *"It is required of stewards that one be found trustworthy"* (1 Corinthians 4.2).

Our children and grandchildren belong to God. We are simply given a stewardship over them for a few years. So, we must make the most of every opportunity to instill a God-confidence in their hearts. That takes time and consistency on our part as we share God's Word and our experiences with the generations behind us. But younger people today are living in such a fast-paced, topsy-turvy world that it's easy to feel like we're being left behind. That's why one of the temptations for us is to dump all of our wisdom on them in one big load.

But that's not the way it works. True discipleship and spiritual formation cannot be fast-tracked. The wisdom and insight we have gained has been a lifelong process. It's vital that we don't forget what we have learned and are still learning, so we can communicate God's Word and His work in our lives to others. Moses said to the generation of Israelites about to enter the promised land, *"Only give heed to yourself and keep your soul diligently,* **so that you do not forget the things which your eyes have seen and they do not depart from your heart all the days of your life;** *but make them known to your sons and your grandsons"* (Deuteronomy 4.9).

This verse speaks to lifelong learning and teaching, the investment in others' lives that the New Testament calls making disciples. It's not sitting someone down for an hour-long lecture, but building on God's truth one day at a time. Moses explained the process in this classic passage, which I want to quote in its entirety because it is so clear:

> *You shall love the* L<small>ORD</small> *your God with all your heart and with all your soul and with all your might. These words, which I am commanding you today, shall be on your heart. You shall teach them diligently to your sons and shall talk of them when you sit in your house and when you walk by the way and when you lie down and when you rise up.*

You shall bind them as a sign on your hand and they shall be as frontals on your forehead. You shall write them on the doorposts of your house and on your gates. Deuteronomy 6.5–9

When children are at home, we have many opportunities to talk about the things of God at mealtimes, and when they go to bed and get up. Those days are far behind for Vicki and me, so the best things we can do for our adult children, and other younger people in our sphere of influence, is to let them know how special they are; to pay attention to what they're experiencing; to let them know we love and are praying for them; to tell them how we see God working in their lives; and to encourage them in their parenting and workplaces.

What I'm saying is that we don't have to be relationship experts to be good spiritual investors. We just need to pray and listen and watch. Vicki and I live in the Dallas area. Our daughter in California is raising four kids. Everything about their lives is different than the world in which we raised her. So, I just want to say to her, "Sweetheart, I love you. Tell me about the stress that you're under in your home. Tell me about the good things God is doing, because I want to pray for you."

I may not use the word "invest" with her, but I want to invest my life in what she and my two other adult children are doing, so that they're in a better position to do what God has called them to do in their families, churches, and communities. I want to encourage them and others in the generations following me to know how much we love them and are their cheerleaders, and to help them catch a glimpse of how much God wants to do with them in their world.

Let me emphasize here again that while for most of us, investing in future generations involves primarily our children and grandchildren, we can also have a much wider sphere of influence for Christ if we will just look around us and allow God to point out people we can interact with. I have a six-year-old friend whose family moved into our neighborhood. I spoke to another new neighbor across the alley who is a retired pastor. It has developed into a wonderful friendship. I mention him on purpose because investing in people's lives doesn't have to be limited to those younger than we are.

In other words, your sphere of influence might be wider than you imagine. And it isn't always through a long-term relationship. Your impact can have an immediate effect on someone God puts in your path. Jesus taught us this truth in His famous parable of the Good Samaritan (Luke 19.25–37). The Samaritan interrupted his day and went out of his way to care for the man who had been left for dead by robbers. He also dug into his pocket to pay for the man's room, and was ready to pay more on his way back.

That's a perfect illustration of the cost we may have to pay to influence others. If we are going to be available for God to use us in people's lives, we may need to change our schedule sometimes. We may need to call and say we'll be late to that meeting. We may have to miss a flight because God has put somebody in our lives we need to pay attention to. The amazing thing is that God can use us this way even when we are in a bad place ourselves.

That's clear in 2 Kings 5, the story of the girl who had been taken captive by the Syrians and was a slave in the house of Naaman, the valiant commander of the mighty Syrian army. Naaman had leprosy, which meant isolation from everyone and everything in those days. This slave girl could have said, "Good, that's what he deserves for being an enemy of Israel and taking me captive." But instead, she sent Naaman to the prophet Elisha, who healed him. Naaman went home a believer in the true God. That girl realized that God had put her in Syria to influence those in her sphere for Him.

The Importance of Making Disciples

Vicki and I had a long-time friend who died in his early 90s after a long battle with cancer. I was to officiate at his graveside service, so his widow said she wanted to open the service to any of the grandchildren who wanted to say something about their grandfather.

One of the grandchildren said, "Whenever I went to my grandparents' home, I knew that I was loved and accepted, and I knew I would feel that. And whenever I was in troubled times, I would always find my way back to their house, because I knew that their home and their relationship was a safe place." These grandchildren had seen their grandfather and grandmother love each other faithfully, serve others unselfishly, and give their lives to their family. In other words, my friend and his wife had made disciples of their grandchildren.

My friend, for believers in Jesus Christ making disciples is not optional. Discipleship is adult education, so how can we, as aging Christians, keep making disciples today? Paul gave a wonderful plan for this: *"You therefore, my son, be strong in the grace that is in Christ Jesus. The things which you have heard from me in the presence of many witnesses, entrust these to faithful men who will be able to teach others also"* (2 Timothy 2.1–2).

In just two verses Paul listed at least three generations of disciplers and disciples who can impact others with the teaching of God's Word. And by the way, even as the elders of today's generation, you and I also need to be disciples. Who is discipling you? It doesn't have to be someone older; it can be your pastor or other faithful Bible teacher, or even someone no longer here whose life and example are still inspiring others.

One of our professors at Dallas Theological seminary told his class, "So you want to be discipled? Go to the library and read the works of great theologians and Bible teachers who have gone before us. Read the biographies of great missionaries."

I mention that to remind you and myself that one exciting aspect of our disciple-making is that our influence can and will outlive us in the generations that follow us. Here are the generations generally recognized over the past century:

- Silent Generation 1910-26
- Greatest Generation 1927-45
- Baby Boomers 1946-62
- Generation X 1963-81
- Millennials 1982-2000
- Generation Z 2001-19

- iGeneration 2007-present (defined as the iPhone generation)

As we consider these generations, especially the ones coming after us, we also need to be reminded that the church is a wonderful, God-ordained place to make disciples. Since the church is a multigenerational organism—a living entity, not just a building or organization—investing into the generations that follow and surround us is a critical assignment for both life and church leadership.

We hear a lot about dreams today. Everyone is telling the young generation to follow their dreams. That's fine, but the only dreams truly worth following are God's dreams for us and our families. The apostle Peter recounted an amazing prophecy from the book of Joel on the Day of Pentecost, the church's birthday:

*AND IT SHALL BE IN THE LAST DAYS, God says, THAT I WILL POUR FORTH OF MY SPIRIT ON ALL MANKIND; AND YOUR SONS AND YOUR DAUGHTERS SHALL PROPHESY, AND YOUR YOUNG MEN SHALL SEE VISIONS, AND **YOUR OLD MEN SHALL DREAM DREAMS.*** Acts 2.17

Here is a great prophecy that would be fulfilled in the ministry of the church. What's interesting is that the prophecy says it is the "old men," the aging generation, who would "dream dreams." "Dreams" is not a word we hear a lot in relation to elderly people, but we need to be dreaming dreams of what God wants to do in the lives of our adult children and grandchildren, and the life of the church. The Holy Spirit calls older and younger generations to work together in building Christ's church. The question is, are we doing that as the old men and women in our churches and families?

The Importance of Mentoring

As we invest in generations following us, I believe that intentional, relational mentoring is critically important. By that I mean providing an example for others to follow. Relational mentoring is that which happens when our lives are interwoven with others. That makes mentoring a key part of discipleship.

Dennis Rainey has written a great book entitled, *Stepping Up: A Call to Courageous Manhood.* He lists five stages of manhood, but I only want to focus on the last two stages which address retiring Boomers and seniors, who are the focus of FWM. (While Rainey's book is addressed to men, I believe these principles apply equally well to women.)

Rainey's fourth stage is Mentor. He writes: "A mentor is a life coach—a tutor and instructor who recognizes that he has the privilege and duty of passing a baton in a generational relay race. Stepping up and becoming a mentor can be one of the most definitive and courageous steps a man makes in his lifetime.

"Every man needs a mentor, and every man needs to BE a mentor. We need another man to speak into our lives, cheering us on, imparting the courage to persevere, summoning us to keep stepping up. In turn, we need to mentor others. This is our generational responsibility" (p. 147).

"A mentor purposely builds life lessons into those he mentors. As you consider being a mentor, think through what makes life work for you—at work, at home, and in your relationship with Christ. What have you learned about the following?

- Handling pressure and balancing the pace of life
- Working with people
- Building and keeping friendships with other men/women
- Investing in your marriage
- Resolving conflict
- Facing unexpected crises or tragedy
- Managing your finances
- Developing a real relationship with God
- Reading, understanding, and applying the Scriptures
- Raising your children
- Developing the type of character needed to succeed at work
- Growing through failure" (see Rainey, *Stepping Up*, pp.157-158).

Remember, reaching retirement age does not mean for one moment that we have the luxury of not continuing to pour our lives out for the generation following us. God calls every disciple to continue giving his or her life away for the blessing and encouragement of others.

In what ways might you consider the invitation and challenge of being a mentor to the younger generations around you in your church or community? Consider these additional ideas for mentoring, taken from **Vantagepoint3.org** (a wonderful mentoring ministry).

Mentoring: How daunting is the thought of becoming someone's mentor?

Breaking the sometimes-daunting perception of mentoring into smaller pieces can help us recognize the variety of ways mentoring happens.

- **Disciplers** help to develop basic skills for knowing and following Jesus.
- **Spiritual mentors** help others pay attention to the movement of God in their lives.
- **Coaches** help develop skills and motivate people in real-life situations.
- **Counselors** provide presence, processing, and clarifying perspectives.
- **Teachers** help provide knowledge and motivation for other's learning.
- **Sponsors** advocate for developing younger people or organizations.

Consider how God has led you and shaped your life to impact others, and then answer this question: How have you been uniquely wired to pay attention to and companion with others?

John Wooden at UCLA was without a doubt the most successful college basketball coach ever. One of his stars was the basketball legend Kareem Abdul-Jabbar, who played for Coach Wooden in the 1970s. Jabbar was a black kid from Brooklyn, and Wooden was an older white man.

But they formed a special bond that was very touching to see fifty years later when they held an event to honor Coach Wooden, now elderly and unsteady. He came up leaning on the arm of Abdul-Jabbar, a reversal of their roles decades earlier when Jabbar leaned on Wooden as his coach and father figure.

John Wooden once said, "While I made my living as a coach, I have lived my life to be a mentor, and to be mentored! Constantly. Everything in the world has been passed down. Every piece of knowledge is something that has been shared by someone else. If you understand it as I do, mentoring becomes your true legacy. It is the greatest inheritance you can give others. It is why you get up every day—to teach and to be taught."

For Further Thinking

I hope this study has inspired you and given you concrete examples and ideas for how you can invest your life in the lives of others, especially those in the future generations. Here are some final thoughts and verses to further help your thinking and study of this fourth essential. These biblical passages speak to the importance of transitions from one generation to the next generation. Read through them and take notes as to what they teach as it relates to a person's final days in life and passing the truth of God from one generation to the next:

- Genesis 48–50: Jacob and Joseph
- Deuteronomy 31–34: Moses

- Joshua 24: Joshua
- 1 Chronicles 28–29: David and Solomon
- John 13–17: Jesus and His disciples (His entire Upper Room Discourse)
- 2 Timothy: Paul and Timothy

Here are some ideas from a group study on how and where we can begin the process of investing our lives in discipling and mentoring others:

- Our families
- Friends at church
- Friends in our community/profession
- Show an interest
- Invite them to your home for a meal
- Share your history/story
- Write them
- Pray for them
- Text/call
- Common interests—share your interests

Before we close, we need to ask an important question that should be considered: How does Satan work to keep us from investing in others? We've considered some potential barriers to doing this, such as the feeling that we have nothing to contribute, or that no one is interested in what we have to say. As you consider your calling in this area, be alert for ways that the enemy of our souls can work to discourage and dissuade you—and don't give in to him!

Allow me a few closing thoughts. I would not be where I am now without older people who have encouraged me and poured their lives into me, beginning with my high school days right up to today. One thing I can do is to thank them, and the second thing I can do is to follow their example and pour my life into others coming behind me.

I am forever indebted to the men and women who have helped me become the man, husband, father, and friend I am today. I am not a self-made man by any stretch! None of us is. God has worked in our lives through other people. And the best gift we can give back to Him is to do the same for them.

CHAPTER FIVE

The Fifth Essential:
The Importance of Being Available

"Always be ready for the next thing." Don Guthrie

"Nearly all the best things that came to me in life have been unexpected and unplanned by me." Carl Sandburg

Being available simply means being open to new ways and new people through which God wants to lead and move in our lives to accomplish His purposes for us. He often leads in ways we might never have dreamt, which is why we often wonder what God is up to. He knows our tomorrows, and He has a plan for us that will involve new things and new people. But since we don't know what tomorrow or the next day will bring, the best thing we can do is to be available for God to lead and use us.

The psalmist wrote,

"This is the day which the LORD *has made; let us rejoice and be glad in it"* (Psalm 118.24). That's a great way to begin every day, anticipating that whatever comes this day has been designed by God for your good. Someone has said it's not your abilities God wants to work through so much as your availability. So first of all, and above all, this *Fifth Essential for Finishing Well* means being available to God for His presence and work in our lives.

God's Leading in My Life

I hope you'll be encouraged by my story of how God has led and shaped my life as I have sought to be available to His leading-and how He continues to do so in new and exciting ways in my aging years. This *Seven Essentials for Finishing Well* series, and FWM itself, are Exhibit A of how God wanted to use me to help and encourage other seniors as I finished my pastoral ministry and God opened this new door of service.

I can look back and see how God determined the path of my life from the very beginning. He determined the home into which I was born in Hershey, Pennsylvania. That was so crucial because it was through my home and my local church that I trusted Christ as my Savior at the age of six. My high school years were incredibly formative for my spiritual life, and then I attended Taylor University, a Christian school in Indiana, following an older brother.

From there, God led me to Dallas Theological Seminary through a missionary I met while serving in Haiti on a summer mission project. I met my wife, Vicki, in Dallas through a blind date set up by a close friend. I taught the Medical-Dental Sunday School class of physicians and dentists for five years, and through that I was introduced to a ministry whose work was with Christian physicians and dentists (the Christian Medical and Dental Associations). Vicki and I served together in CMDA for fourteen years. Then, through friends I had first met in that Medical-Dental Sunday school class, I pastored Dallas Bible Church for over twenty-one years.

FWM *was* then born out of a network of friendships in that church. It may seem as though these events were random, but I believe that God works through so-called random events. I am where I am today because of how the sovereign hand of God has led me all these years. I am also who I am because of the people I've met and experiences I've had that changed me and the course of my life.

I didn't plan it that way. I had no idea how my life would unfold, *but God did*! He led me through all the above, and He keeps leading me now in the same ways through my aging years. The constant key is being available to the leadership of God in my life.

Examples of Being Available

I want to encourage you right up front with three wonderful examples of being available—two from the Scriptures and one from today. You may be familiar with Jesus' story of the Good Samaritan (Luke 10.25–37), which we have alluded to before. As the Samaritan was on his journey one day, he didn't expect to find that man who had been robbed, beaten, and left for dead by thieves. A priest and a Levite, religious leaders in Israel, passed by but didn't stop because they were occupied by their duties, and perhaps afraid to get involved.

But the Samaritan was available to have his day and his life redirected to serve someone who needed him, even at his own expense. Jesus told that parable to teach us that anyone who needs us is our "neighbor," and we must be available to help. And notice that the Samaritan didn't have any particular skills for this assignment, just a caring heart that was willing to be interrupted and inconvenienced.

A second example of being available for God to work through unforeseen events is the birth of Jesus (Luke 2.1–7). Joseph and Mary had nothing to do with a census order being issued from Rome that required them to travel to Bethlehem, Joseph's family home, to be registered. Mary didn't expect to be visited by an angel with an announcement that to her seemed impossible (Luke 1.26–38), and Joseph certainly didn't expect his future wife to be pregnant. But both of them made themselves available to God not only for the birth of our Savior, but also for the fulfillment of many prophecies about Jesus' birth, including the fact that He would be born in Bethlehem (Micah 5.2) even though Joseph and Mary didn't live there.

My modern-day story comes from a group I led in a study of the *Seven Essentials* at a church in Dallas. One man was an hour late to the study one morning. He said he had had a car accident, and it turned out the other driver was a fellow believer. My friend got to talking with him, and discovered that this man was searching for God's will in his life. My friend brought this man to our study, and he became part of our group.

It's almost crazy how God orchestrates life sometimes in ways we would never expect. The accident was unfortunate and inconvenient, but my friend didn't let that stop him from being sensitive and open to God's leading.

God's Promises to the Available

The truly exciting thing about making ourselves available to God is that He doesn't just throw us out there into life's circumstances and expect us to discern on our own what He wants us to do. He has promised us His guidance each day, as stated in this classis passage: *"Trust in the LORD with all your heart and do not lean on your own understanding. In all your ways acknowledge Him, and He will make your paths straight"* (Proverbs 3.5–6).

We need this guidance because, as I said above, we can't figure out life. I would have never, ever guessed that I'd live in Dallas. It was one of God's surprises. I don't know where the next ten or twenty years will take me, if I am still here.

But I know that God has a plan He's working. So, the wisest course for me is to trust Him and be ready for what He wants to do with me. This is so important because I can't see around the next bend. I can't see around the curve of cancer or disappointment. But God can, and He makes my paths straight even when life bends around a curve. I hope that rings true in your life as well. Think back over your life and reflect on the ways God has led you and straightened some crooked paths to bring you to where you are today.

As we've already seen, sometimes being available means being willing to get up from where we are and go to a new place—even if it's someplace we've never been before and aren't completely sure about. I want to quote God's call to Abram to leave his comfortable life in the highly civilized region called "Ur of the Chaldeans" (Genesis 11.31) and go to the land of Canaan on nothing but God's assurance of future blessing:

> *Now the* LORD *said to Abram, "Go forth from your country, and from your relatives and from your father's house, to the land which I will show you; and I will make you a great nation, and I will bless you, and make your name great; and so you shall be a blessing."* Genesis 12.1–2

The story goes on to reveal that God did bless and prosper Abram in the Promised Land, changing nis name to Abraham as a symbol of his future role as father of the Jewish nation. But I want you to see that Abram didn't know all of that when he took his family from Ur to Canaan. And lest we think Abraham's response to God's surprising leading was a life of ease and luxury in Canaan, the writer of Hebrews tells us that Abraham *"lived as an alien in the land of promise, as in a foreign land, dwelling in tents with Isaac and Jacob, fellow heirs of the same promise"* (Hebrews 11.9). God showed Abraham the future *by faith*, and Abraham moved out.

At other times, availability to God involves fear of a threat or danger. This was the case for Joshua as he inherited the leadership of Israel from Moses and prepared to lead the people into the Promised Land that was inhabited by fearsome enemies. We'll talk more about fear below as a barrier to being available to God.

But for now, notice the theme of Moses's final message to the people as they stood at the border of Canaan:

Be strong and courageous, **do not be afraid or tremble at them***, for the* LORD *your God is the one who goes with you. He will not fail you or forsake you." Then Moses called to Joshua and said to him in the sight of all Israel, "***Be strong and courageous****. . . . The* LORD *is the one who goes ahead of you; He will be with you. He will not fail you or forsake you.* ***Do not fear*** *or be dismayed.* Deuteronomy 31.6–8

Even a leader as mighty as Joshua felt fearful at the task before him of conquering Canaan. But God had a plan and a promise for Joshua, who overcame his fear and led the people of Israel into the Promised Land.

God's Plan for You and Me

You may read all of this and say, "Sure, God had a plan for people like Joseph, Mary, Moses, and Joshua. They were chosen to accomplish great things for God. Moses and Joshua were mighty leaders of God's chosen people. I'm not in that category."

Neither am I, but I want you to know that God has outlined a life plan for you and me that is as important for us as His plan was for the great figures of the Bible. Psalm 139.16 is often quoted, and rightly so, in defense of the unborn. But read it again with our aging years in mind: *"Your eyes have seen my unformed substance; and in Your book were all written the days that were ordained for me, when as yet there was not one of them."*

Think about the impact of that verse at our stage of life. God cares for us so fully and intimately that He "ordained," set aside, a plan for us that covers *all* of our days. That truth has tremendous implications for us in our aging years. God is still unfolding and revealing His good plan for us today every bit as much as He did when we were in the full bloom of youth!

So instead of sitting back and saying, "Well, I've already had my last rodeo," or living only in a "safe" zone with what we know or are good at, we can open ourselves to new possibilities and adventures God has for us. All that's required is our availability to God and those around us. And to reinforce the truth that God has a good plan for us, Jesus said, *"You did not choose Me but I chose you, and appointed you that you would go and bear fruit, and that your fruit would remain"* (John 15.16).

I love what the psalmist wrote about the impact that we as God's people can have in our aging years:

> *The righteous man will flourish like the palm tree, he will grow like a cedar in Lebanon. Planted in the house of the* LORD, *they will flourish in the courts of our God. They will still yield fruit in old age; they shall be full of sap and very green, to declare that the* LORD *is upright; He is my rock, and there is no unrighteousness in Him.* Psalm 92.12–15

As Robert Browning wrote of these years, "The best is yet to be." That's so true for God's people, those who are following Jesus. Paul wrote: *"Those who are led by the Spirit of God are the sons of God"* (Romans 8.14). The Holy Spirit has a plan for us. My questions for you are the ones I ask myself: Am I available to the Spirit for His purposes today? Do I daily seek His leadership, both in the big things and in my daily routines of life? If you can say yes to these, you're ready for God to use.

The apostle Peter pointed to Jesus as an example of this truth when he said of the Lord, **"He went about doing good"** (Acts 10.38). Jesus was always available for the people His Father brought into His life.

Should it be any different for you and me? Paul didn't think so, which is why he wrote: *"Let us not lose heart in doing good, for in due time we will reap if we do not grow weary. So then, while we have opportunity,* **let us do good to all people***, and especially to those who are of the household of the faith"* (Galatians 6.9–10).

When Jesus called His disciples, He said to them, *"From now on you will be catching men"* (Luke 5.10) instead of fish. He was referring to the ministry of sharing the Gospel, which we are also called to do. We could say this requires the ultimate in availability, since many opportunities for a Gospel witness arise when we're aren't expecting them. But when we're praying and asking God to make us aware of those around us in a new way, He will help us see the world through new eyes—the eyes of Jesus.

Dietrich Bonhoeffer wisely wrote, "We must be ready to allow ourselves to be interrupted by God. God will be constantly crossing our paths and canceling our plans by sending us people with claims and petitions." He went on to say how important it is that we not pass them by, but stop to help as the Samaritan did.

A Plan for Being Available

Even though the essence of being available is simply being ready for the circumstances and, especially the people, God brings into our lives; the kind of availability we're talking about doesn't happen by accident. Here's a simple plan that may help you be ready for those "kingdom opportunities":

1. Open your mind. By that I simply mean making a conscious effort to be aware of the people and situations around you with the goal of being available as God may lead. It's very tempting for us at our age to stay in our comfort zone. Being willing to take a risk and make a sacrifice may sound a little scary, but it will take us beyond our personal plans and self-goals, which can become all-important if we're not careful.

2. Listen with intentionality. Ours is a very noisy and distracting world. But when you're alert to God's work, you'll discover that people reveal a lot about their needs and what is going on inside them by what they say.

3. See with your spiritual eyes. This is the other side of listening with intentionality. Paul prayed for believers that *"the eyes of your heart may be enlightened"* (Ephesians 1:18).

As followers of Jesus, we are called to see people the way He saw them; not simply noting—or even ignoring—their presence and passing by, but really seeing them with the goal of helping them where needed.

4. Open your heart. This is where intent meets action! It's where being available may cost you something as you reach out to meet a need. But the rewards and blessings far outweigh any cost.

This is the challenge to each of us as we age. Will we be the kind of men and women who will simply say "Yes' to the opportunities God keeps placing before us in our aging years? God will do great things in and through us if we are alert to Him.

Barriers to Being Available

I'm sure you've seen those dramas in which a fugitive is fleeing and the police have set up a roadblock. There's usually an officer standing behind those barriers waving his arms for the car to stop. Everything about that scene says, "Stop! Don't even try to go on! That would be a bad idea!"

That's the scene I want you to visualize as we close this study. We've mentioned several barriers to availability, which can be intimidating. And behind those barriers is someone waving his arms to stop us in our tracks. That someone is Satan, the sworn enemy of our souls. He can throw up all kinds of fears and suggestions to keep us wrapped up in ourselves and our aches and pains and complaints. Here are some other barriers one of our study groups came up with:

- Fear of failure or rejection
- Unwillingness to yield; stubbornness
- Time; hurriedness
- Procrastination
- Lack of awareness
- Unforgiveness/bitterness
- Lack of curiosity or lack of grace
- Lack of teachability; set in our ways, "never done it that way before"

A Closing Story

That's a pretty formidable list, but we can overcome any or all of these in the power of the Holy Spirit. Let me close with an inspirational story of a person who was alert and available at a crucial moment, and changed a little boy's life. It has made a deep impression on me.

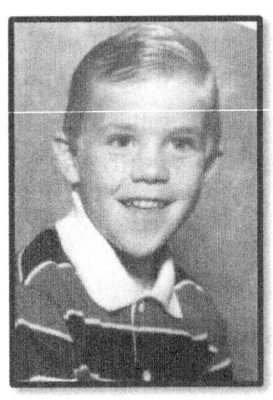

John Gilbert was diagnosed with Duchenne's Muscular Dystrophy at the age of five. When he was about eight years old, he was the poster child for muscular dystrophy in California and attended a fundraiser/auction for MD in Sacramento.

The fundraiser was sponsored by the National Football League, and therefore oriented to athletic items. Though he was wheelchair bound, John raised his hand to bid on a basketball that was autographed by every player of the Sacramento Kings pro basketball team. He said later that he never felt so many G forces as when his mother pushed his hand back down, since they had no money for an object like this.

For some unexplainable reason, the bidding on the basketball continued to rise until the price was quite high. Finally, the auctioneer said "Sold," and looked at a gentleman across the room to come and receive his purchase. The man came to receive the ball, but he did not return to his seat. Instead, he turned and walked across the room to where John was in his wheelchair and gave him the ball.

This man had noticed John's desire and gave of himself and his resources to meet John's need. He was *available* for a greater cause at a particular time on that particular day. (*From Eden to Paradise: Something Stronger Than Time, An Autobiography by John Stuart Gilbert, A Father's Reflections* by Bruce Stuart Gilbert, Xulon Press, 2012, pp. 77-79.)

I want to be like that. I want to be available to the Spirit of God for something new that I've never thought about before. Satan knocks on my door and says "Habecker, don't open yourself to something new. It could be risky. Just do what you're already good at. Don't venture out."

But that's not what the life of faith is all about. I go back to the *First Essential* which says we will grow and not stay the same. I want to be available to God. I want to keep growing. I want to keep connecting. I want to keep loving. I want to keep investing. Join me in this great adventure!

CHAPTER SIX

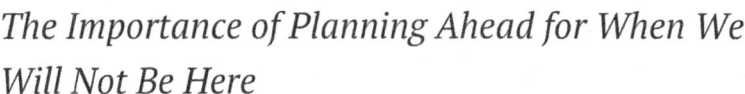

The Sixth Essential:

The Importance of Planning Ahead for When We Will Not Be Here

---

"Death is no more than passing from one room into another. But there's a difference for me, you know. Because in that other room I shall be able to see." –Helen Keller

"I am not tired of my work, neither am I tired of the world; yet, when Christ calls me home, I shall go with gladness." –Adoniram Judson

"Growing, ripening, aging, dying—the passing of time is predestined, inevitable. There is only one solution if old age is not to be an absurd parody of our former life, and that is to go on pursuing ends that give our existence a meaning—devotion to individuals, to groups or to causes, social, political, intellectual or creative work. . . . In old age we should wish still to have passions strong enough to prevent us turning in on ourselves. One's life has value so long as one attributes value to the life of others, by means of love, friendship, indignation, compassion." –Simone de Beauvoir in The Coming of Age

"William Hazlitt wrote that no young man believes that he will ever die, and the truth of the matter, I think, is that in some measure that is true of all men. Intellectually we all know that we will die, but we do not really know it in the sense that the knowledge becomes part of us. We do not really know it in the sense of living as though it were true. On the contrary, we tend to live as though our lives would go on forever. We spend our lives like drunken sailors." (Frederick Buechner in The Hungering Dark)

I realize that talking about the end of life and planning ahead for the time when we will not be here is an uncomfortable subject for many people, perhaps even considered morbid. But that's not what we are about here at all! Most people want to leave a good legacy for their loved ones, and believers in Christ should be at the head of that list. In fact, the Scriptures tell us, *"A good man leaves an inheritance to his children's children"* (Proverbs 13.22). That's what I want to do, and I believe you do too. As we'll see, the Bible is as clear and forthright about the end of life as it is about birth and all the stages in between.

Leaving a Legacy

Nothing would give me greater joy than knowing that my influence for Christ will outlast me. I want to continue impacting the generations that follow me after I'm gone. And as a husband, father, and grandfather, I want to pass on to my family and to God's work the material goods He has blessed me with, to help sustain my family and the work of the Gospel for years to come. My tombstone will have my date of birth in 1949 and, as least for now, the dash. I don't know what that end date will be, even as is true for you. God gives us indications as we age, and we know for sure we are closer to that time today than we were yesterday.

God's Word on Our Last Days

The Scriptures urge us to look at the end of life not just as "pie in the sky, by and by," but as a reality that needs to be addressed, and as a motivator to live life for God to the fullest now. I'm amazed at how much the Bible speaks of death—both of its inevitability and the importance of preparing for it. I've selected just a few of these many passages that highlight this point.

The writer of the book of Ecclesiastes was Solomon, the wisest man who ever lived. His life is a classic example of our subject, for several reasons. He reached the pinnacle of wealth and success as the king of Israel, but to say that he did not finish well is an understatement. His demise is recorded in 1 Kings 11, a case study in how not to prepare well for the end of life.

Solomon apparently wrote Ecclesiastes during those bitter older years, but it contains a wealth of wisdom on life that we can learn from. He famously wrote, *"There is an appointed time for everything. And there is a time for every event under heaven—a time to give birth and a time to die"* (Ecclesiastes 3.1–2). That says in beautiful poetic form what I am urging you to consider in this *Sixth Essential*.

Based on this inescapable truth, Solomon went on to give us some very wise advice that may sound gloomy at first. But

I find it very encouraging to help me think about what's important in life and how to have an end-of-life mindset that prepares us to live well today and every day:

> *The day of one's death is better than the day of one's birth. It is better to go to a house of mourning than to go to a house of feasting, because that is the end of every man, and the living takes it to heart. Sorrow is better than laughter, for when a face is sad a heart may be happy. The mind of the wise is in the house of mourning, while the mind of fools is in the house of pleasure.* Ecclesiastes 7.1–4

Think about what Solomon is saying and *not* saying. He is not saying we should spend our days in funeral homes, or go about with gloomy faces. But as one who had known the heights and the follies of worldly pleasure, Solomon urged us to live with the end of life in mind.

That's the point of this essential; to take account of the end of our lives and then work backward to today. The person who does this will have both his earthly and heavenly affairs in order when his life ends. Think about how wise that is, both for you and your loved ones. I've performed many funerals as a pastor. The reason so many people are very uncomfortable at funerals is not just grief for the deceased, but because they don't like thinking about death or being around it, and they can't wait to get out of there and get on with their lives.

That's understandable in one sense. But God's Word says that the person who lives only for the present with no thought to tomorrow is not wise. And to cement his point, Solomon began the last chapter of Ecclesiastes with this counsel: *"Remember also your Creator in the days of your youth, before the evil days come and the years draw near when you will say, 'I have no delight in them'"* (Ecclesiastes 12.1). The rest of that chapter is a poetic description of the aging process with its aches and limitations.

Now you may read this and say, "But I'm not a youth anymore. I'm in this aging process. Is Solomon saying it's too late for me to plan on finishing well?" Of course not! The wonderful thing about our gracious God is that He meets us where we are and takes us from there. If I thought it was too late, I would never have started this ministry!

On the contrary, this is the right time for us to ensure, to the best of our ability, that we are planning wisely for when we will not be here. That certainly includes our financial estate, but planning wisely from God's perspective is much more than that. It's possible to amass a fortune and still end life in frustration, as David explained in these important verses:

> **L**ORD**, make me to know my end and what is the extent of my days***; let me know how transient I am. Behold, You have made my days as handbreadths, and my lifetime as nothing in Your sight; surely every man at his best is a mere breath. Selah. Surely every man walks about as a phantom;*

surely they make an uproar for nothing; **he amasses riches and does not know who will gather them.** Psalm 39.4–6

David spoke very eloquently here about both the brevity of life and the importance of finishing well from God's perspective. I love David's prayer for God to keep him aware that his days were numbered. Again, that's not a morbid statement for a believer. It's simply another reminder that all of our days are written in God's book.

Planning Today for Tomorrow

Since this is true, the best way to prepare for death is to go to the end of life and plan backwards. David's last statement is an example of why planning well financially is not enough by itself to truly finish well from the standpoint of eternity. The reason is that we will leave all we have gained to those who come behind us, and we can't guarantee that they will handle our hard-earned resources wisely (read Ecclesiastes 2.18–19 for a forceful statement on that).

The Psalms are so packed with godly wisdom that I want to show you two more passages. The psalmist asked, *"Why should I fear in days of adversity?"* (Psalm 49:5). He goes to explain the foolishness of *"those who trust in their wealth and boast in the abundance of their riches"* (v. 6), thinking that these things can protect them from life's hard times and assure them of long life now and salvation at the end of life. The writer then offers these powerful truths:

> *Even wise men die; the stupid and the senseless alike perish and leave their wealth to others. Their inner thought is that their houses are forever and their dwelling places to all generations; they have called their lands after their own names. But man in his pomp will not endure; he is like the beasts that perish.* Psalm 49.10–12

Psalm 90 was written by Moses, who was not only a very wise man but learned the importance of finishing well—the hard way. If you know your Bible history, Moses disobeyed God when he got angry at the complaining Israelites and struck the rock in the desert for water instead of speaking to it as God commanded him. Moses' punishment for this disobedience was to not be allowed to lead the Israelites into the Promised Land, but only view it from a distance (Numbers 20.6–12; Deuteronomy 34.1–5).

Imagine how hard this judgment was for the man who had freed God's people from slavery in Egypt and put up with their griping and rebellion for forty years. Moses died seeing the land his heart longed for, but he could not enter it. I mention this because Moses' end-of-life experience makes a tremendous backdrop for his counsel in Psalm 90:

> *All our days have declined in Your fury; we have finished our years like a sigh. As for the days of our life, they contain seventy years, or if due to strength, eighty years, yet their pride is but labor and sorrow; for soon it is gone and we fly away. Who understands the power of Your anger and*

Your fury, according to the fear that is due You? **So teach us to number our days, that we may present to You a heart of wisdom.** Psalm 90.9–12

What a passionate plea to plan for when we will not be here! We've already learned that God has numbered our days, so Moses' prayer is great advice for us.

Additional Thoughts

I love these thoughts that pastor and author Tim Challies, contributes when thinking about death:

> *In reading the Puritans and their successors, I've often come across a captivating little phrase: 'knocking at the gates of the grave.' Jeremy Taylor wrote a whole book about Christian dying and said, 'He that would die well must always look for death, every day knocking at the gates of the grave; and then the gates of the grave shall never prevail against him to do him mischief.' Theodore Cuyler sometimes recounted strolling through Greenwood cemetery where three of his children had been laid to rest—two as infants and one as a young adult—and using his time there to metaphorically knock at the gates of the grave, 'to listen whether any painful echo comes back from within.'*
>
> *We, too, should make it our habit to knock at the gates of the grave. To knock at the gates of the grave is to ponder the positive marks of grace that*

are associated with those who love the Lord and will depart this life to be with him forever. It is to ponder the marks of depravity and hypocrisy that are associated with those who hate the Lord and will depart this life to be separated from him forever. It is to heed the admonition of the Apostle who implored Christians to 'examine yourselves, to see whether you are in the faith. Test yourselves. Or do you not realize this about yourselves, that Jesus Christ is in you? - unless indeed you fail to meet the test! 2 Corinthians 13:5

We knock when we pray, 'Search me, O God, and know my heart! Try me and know my thoughts! And see if there be any grievous way in me and lead me in the way everlasting' (Psalm 139:23–24)! We knock when we cry to God, 'Prove me, O LORD, and try me; test my heart and my mind. For your steadfast love is before my eyes, and I walk in your faithfulness' (Psalm 26:2–3). We knock when we prepare to celebrate the Lord's Supper and examine ourselves, and so eat of the bread and drink of the cup (1 Corinthians 11:28). We knock when we consider whether our lives are increasingly marked by those precious evidence of God's saving and sanctifying grace.

When we knock at the gates of the grave in these ways and many others, we meditatively listen to hear the distant echoes of the choir of angels or the distant echoes of the gavel of judgment. We knock

> *and then listen for echoes that are encouraging or concerning, delightful or painful. We knock and listen so we are prepared for the day—the inevitable day—when the gates will open to receive us to new life or a second death, to the bliss of heaven or the horrors of hell. We knock to ensure we are waiting, to ensure we are ready, to ensure we will go to be with the Lord we love.* (Tim Challies, <u>Do You Knock at the Gates of the Grave?</u>)

This is wise counsel—especially so when you learn that Tim's 20-year-old son, a student in seminary and engaged to be married, collapsed suddenly one day and died. This brother knows whereof he speaks. He's been to "the gates of the grave and knows how important it is to live well and prepare well for the day "when the gates will open to receive us to new life or a second death."

Before we turn to the practical side of preparing for when we won't be here, let me also share this epic poem from John Donne's *Holy Sonnets* which reminds us that death will not have the last word for the believer (we'll look at the subject of eternity in the *Seventh Essential*).

> Death, be not proud, though some have called thee
> Mighty and dreadful, for thou art not so;
> For those whom thou think'st thou dost overthrow
> Die not, poor Death, nor yet canst thou kill me
> From rest and sleep, which but thy pictures be,
> Much pleasure; then from thee much more must flow,
> And soonest our best men with thee do go,

Rest of their bones, and soul's delivery.
Thou art slave to fate, chance, kings, and desperate men,
And dost with poison, war, and sickness dwell,
And poppy or charms can make us sleep as well
And better than thy stroke; why swell'st thou then?
One short sleep past, we wake eternally
And death shall be no more; Death, thou shalt die.

Barriers to Planning Ahead

As we have done with the previous essentials, we need to briefly consider some of the most common barriers that can keep us from making these preparations. These have come from my teaching sessions with people like you, so they are "real-life."

And, also, as we have done with the previous essentials, we should consider how Satan, the enemy of our souls, wants to keep us from planning ahead. Satan may not care so much about the financial estate you leave behind, but he is definitely interested in wrecking your life and testimony, and making sure the fallout continues into future generations.

Satan focuses on this because he knows what God said in Exodus 20.5 about visiting the sins of the father on their descendants for three or four generations. The truth is that Satan is more strategic and multi-generational in his thinking than many Christians. That's one reason I developed these essentials to help God's people prepare well for when they won't be here.

Since this *Sixth Essential* takes us more deeply into personal issues than perhaps the others, I encourage you to think through this list of barriers and identify the things you may encounter as you work through the process, so you won't be taken off-guard when they arise:

- Denial of the reality of death; not learning from the experiences we've had with the issue
- Underestimating our influence; "No one wants to know my history"
- Being self-consumed; so wrapped up in what we're doing that we don't take time to share it
- Painful or uncomfortable moments in our past; especially if not dealt with properly
- Family conflicts; too many touchy subjects better left alone

Planning Ahead for Our Legacy

There are some important checklists below that will help guide you in the important process of planning for when you will not be here. To set the stage, I want to consider the biblical patriarch Joseph because his story is a superb example of planning for one's death. Let me give you the text, then point out several critically important things Joseph did in this process:

> *Now Joseph stayed in Egypt, he and his father's household, and Joseph lived one hundred and ten years. Joseph saw the third generation of Ephraim's sons; also the sons of Machir, the son of Manasseh, were born on Joseph's knees. Joseph said to his brothers, 'I am about to die, but God will surely take care of you and bring you up from this land to the land*

which He promised on oath to Abraham, to Isaac and to Jacob.' Then Joseph made the sons of Israel swear, saying, 'God will surely take care of you, and you shall carry my bones up from here.' So Joseph died at the age of one hundred and ten; and he was embalmed and placed in a coffin in Egypt. Genesis 50.22–26

The first thing Joseph did was put his life in perspective for his family. You may remember that he was sold into slavery in Egypt at the age of 17 and went from prison to second-in-command in Egypt. So, 93 years later when he came to the end of his life, Joseph gathered his sons, grandsons, great-grandsons, and even great-great grandsons to give them his final words of encouragement.

He also extended that message of hope and faith to the nation of Israel. Joseph reminded his family of God's faithfulness both to him and to them by pointing to God's promise to bring them back to the Promised Land. Joseph's request to bring his bones back to Israel was a testimony that God would fulfill His promise.

The second thing Joseph did was make arrangements for the treatment of his body. We often hear Christians say unthinkingly, "Well, I really don't care what you do with my body. I'll be with Jesus, so you can just throw my body on the trash pile if you want."

That may sound spiritual, but actually it's unfair to our loved ones left behind. As a pastor, I've seen families struggle with the issue of bodily burial versus cremation, for example. Cost may decide the issue in the end, but many people feel very strongly about these things when it comes to the treatment of their loved ones.

This and other planning issues are included in the lists below. There are a lot of items here, and you'll want to adapt them to your situation. But myself and the people I've led in numerous seminars agree that these are good basic ideas for planning ahead:

1. Your story. Do your kids and grandkids know your story?

- General biography
- Places lived
- Jobs held
- Highlights
- Hardships, failures, lessons earned
- Consider making a video history

2. People: Who are the people who have influenced you?

- Immediate family lineage; ancestry.com
- Extended family
- Influential people in your life
- Blessing your kids

3. Values: What values have been important to you? Will you pass them on? How?

- What is important to you; your spouse, your marriage?
- What did your parents teach you?
- What did you teach your kids?
- What do you want your kids to teach your grandkids?

4. **Legal Documents: have you taken care of all the legal documents that relate to the end of life one's life?**

- Wills and trusts
- Durable power of attorney
- A medical power of attorney, a living will
- HIPPA release
- Directives to physicians and your family, DNR in and out of the hospital
- Declaration of guardian
- Designation of burial
- Passwords/details related to computer, bank and/or investment details, all the individuals associated with any or all the above
- Kingdom investments; are they reflected in the above?
- Cash available for the immediate future to help family or other details

5. **Funeral Concerns: Are your advanced funeral decisions/directives completed?**

- Burial details
- Disposition of the body; traditional, cremation, body donation
- Pre-planning, funeral directives, advance payment
- Memorial service details; type of memorial service
- Selection of funeral products
- Make them in advance; don't saddle your children with those details
- Writing your own obituary

6. **Pastoral: Conversations/decisions with your spouse and your spiritual leaders**

- Conversations with your pastor
- Memorial service details
- Conversations with your family

7. **Physical: Are you taking care of your health?**

- Regular exercise, staying in shape as best you can
- Decisions that prolong health
- Anticipating and planning for physical hardships
- Long-term care

8. **Spiritual: How will you pass on your spiritual story? Have you written it down? Do your kids know the story of how God has worked in your life?**

- Your spiritual story, how has God led you
- Your spiritual defeats and victories
- Your milestones (Joshua); high points of your life
- People God used in your life
- Preparing for heaven
- Communicating with adult kids (grandkids on appropriate level) in your family about heaven and all the above

One More Important Detail

I want to finish with some thoughts and Scriptures addressing a concern that lingers in the back of the mind for many aging people: **the fear of death.** Death is an event that is ahead for every person. Will we fear it when it comes for us? Will we be ready for it? How might we prepare for death and/or the fear of death emotionally and spiritually?

Take time to examine and think about these important Scriptures. Discuss the texts and think through them line by line or verse-by-verse as you read. What do these passages teach you about death, how to think about it, and life on the other side of death face-to-face with Jesus?

- Psalm 23.4
- 1 Corinthians 15
- John 11
- John 14.1-6
- John 17.20-26
- 2 Corinthians 5.1-10

Also consider these stories of Old Testament saints who prepared for their own deaths and shared those experiences with their families. Study these passages and reflect on how they prepared for their death and how they communicated to those around them. What can you learn from them?

- Jacob: Genesis 48 and 49
- Joseph: Genesis 50
- Joshua: Joshua 24
- Jesus with His disciples: Acts 1.1-11
- Paul: 2 Timothy 4.6-8

Bring up the conversation. Most people don't like to go there, but death is real, and each of us should have a personal degree of comfort in thinking about, preparing for, and initiating conversations with our family and others about death, and specifically about our own death.

Here's one special example. Consider how Moses prepared for his death (Deuteronomy 34.1–12):

- Moses knew the time of his death, and he accepted what God appointed for him.
- Moses knew God face-to-face and trusted Him, even in death.
- God kept His promise to him to show him the land.
- God personally buried him.
- Moses commissioned Joshua, his successor, before he died.
- He was still strong physically when he died.
- He served God faithfully his entire life.

All of these are wonderful but let me leave you with this promise from Scripture **FOR YOU AND ME:** *"Death is swallowed up in victory. O death, where is your victory? O Death, where is your sting? The sting of death is sin, and the power of death is the law; but thanks be to God, who gives us the victory through our Lord Jesus Christ"* (1 Corinthians 15.54–57). Amen!

CHAPTER SEVEN

The Seventh Essential:
The Importance of Anticipating Heaven

"Departures are all alike; it is the landfall that crowns the voyage." C.S. Lewis, in *Letters to Malcolm*.

That's a tremendous truth to think about as we launch into this seventh and final essential for finishing well. Every time I think about heaven, I'm filled with excitement and anticipation. For believers in Christ, heaven is the goal, the home we've been traveling toward all our lives. Even doing this study has increased my excitement and eagerness for heaven, and I hope some of that comes through in the following pages.

The apostle Paul was looking ahead to his "landfall" in heaven as he neared the end of his life. He knew that his final days were fast approaching. What was he anticipating in heaven? We have his answer in Scripture:

> *For I am already being poured out as a drink offering, and the time of my departure has come. I have fought the good fight, I have finished the course, I have kept the faith; in the future there is laid up for me the crown of righteousness, which the Lord, the righteous Judge, will award to me on that day; and not only to me, but also to all who have loved His appearing.* 2 Timothy 4.6–8

Looking Forward to Heaven

We sing about the joy of being in heaven and being reunited with all of our friends and loved ones who have gone before us. I love reunions. When I attended the 50th anniversary reunion of my graduating class at my alma mater, Taylor University, it was great reminiscing and sharing stories with these classmates. Can you imagine doing that in heaven with all the people of God, and seeing Jesus face-to-face? As the song says, what a day that will be!

And yet, my experience is that we don't think very much about our eternal home. When was the last time you had a conversation about heaven? If you're typical of most folks, it was probably at a funeral.

Even though heaven is the ultimate destination and eternal home for every believer, it rarely figures into our daily thoughts and conversations. That's the exact opposite of what we find in Scripture.

Paul was anticipating heaven because it meant eternal life and endless joy with Christ. Paul was so eager for heaven that he said *"to die [in Christ] is gain"* (Philippians 1.21). Then he expressed his great desire *"to depart and be with Christ, for that is very much better"* (v. 23). These verses and the ones above are reminders that as we near the end of life, thinking ahead is critically important.

In one sense, anticipating heaven is like taking a trip to a foreign country. When Vicki and I first went to Italy, we could not read enough to acquaint ourselves with where we would be and what we would see. We read books and studied maps in anticipation of our trip. We made specific plans to see and experience as much as we could while we were in Italy.

After you have an experience like this, a new country doesn't seem nearly so foreign. Maybe that's what Robert Louis Stevenson had in mind when he said, "There are no foreign lands; it is only the traveler that is foreign." Heaven certainly isn't a foreign land to believers in Jesus Christ. It's the perfect home we just haven't experienced yet. In fact, as Christians our true citizenship is already in heaven (Philippians 3.20)! This life is really the "foreign country" for us, a temporary stop on the journey from birth to eternity.

Since heaven is our true home, it makes sense that our hearts would be drawn to it. After all, it won't be long until we're there! The Scriptures also feed our anticipation of heaven and give us many truths to help us prepare for our final journey. That's why I think it's crucial that we invest time thinking through the Bible in anticipation of, and preparation for, heaven—both for ourselves and perhaps for loved ones who may be closer to heaven than we are. We can also celebrate in our spiritual imaginations the joys that the saints of all ages and our departed family members are already experiencing *now* in heaven.

Joyful Scriptures about Heaven

The Bible has so much to say about heaven that I can only include a small sampling in these pages. My goal is to encourage you to anticipate the eternity that believers will spend with Christ. In the previous essential we talked about the importance of going to the end of life and living backward from there. That's still true when it comes to heaven, and even more so.

I hope that these verses will not just stimulate you to dream and daydream about heaven, although that's not a bad idea. But planning ahead for eternity includes living our lives for Christ today in such a way that we *"store up for [our]selves treasure in heaven"* (Matthew 6.20), by which Jesus meant the eternal rewards that He has for those who are faithful to Him.

Turning to Paul again, he explained so well the dilemma we face by trying to imagine what heaven will be like: *"For now we see in a mirror dimly, but then face to face; now I know in part, but then [in heaven] I will know fully just as I also have been fully known"* (1 Corinthians 13.12). We can't see into heaven, which is wise on God's part. That's because if we could, it would probably spoil us for life on earth!

The writers of the Psalms were definitely anticipating the joys of heaven. David wrote: *"You will make known to me the path of life; in Your presence is **fullness of joy**; in Your right hand there are **pleasures forever"*** (Psalm 16.11). This verse alone ought to be enough to get us "pumped" for heaven. We've known joys and pleasures in this life, but not in all their fullness, and certainly not endlessly. But that's exactly what awaits us in heaven.

David finished the most famous Psalm of all with these words: *"Surely goodness and mercy will follow me all the days of my life, and I will dwell in the house of the LORD forever"* (Psalm 23.6). As followers of Christ, we've experienced God's goodness and mercy in abundance along the journey of life. But what will these things look and feel like when we're in the "house of the LORD forever?" I'm not sure, but I'm sure looking forward to it!

The Scriptures also teach that one of the great joys of heaven is that we will have perfect bodies, with all of the pain and tears and failures of earth gone forever. Another psalmist anticipated this: *"My flesh and my heart may fail, but God is the strength of my heart and my portion forever"* (Psalm 73.26). As our bodies deteriorate and weaken in this life (read 2 Corinthians 4.16–18), imagine God being our strength and portion forever. It's mind-boggling.

The night before His crucifixion, Jesus gave His disciples and us tremendous assurance about the reality of heaven, and a tremendous promise of His return to take those who believe in Him to be with Him forever:

> *Do not let your heart be troubled; believe in God, believe also in Me. In My Father's house are many dwelling places; if it were not so I would have told you. For I go to prepare a place for you. And if I go and prepare a place for you, I will come again and receive you to Myself that where I am, there you may be also.* John 14.1–3

Jesus' disciples were troubled in that upper room because He told them He was leaving them. It was a very intense emotional time for them, with several harder days ahead as they watched Him being crucified and buried. But Jesus laid their fears to rest with the promise that He was preparing heaven for them and would bring them there to be with Him forever.

That's a great promise to hold onto, but there is still a sense of mystery about heaven because we don't know everything about it. And as human beings, we tend to shrink back from something mysterious and unknown. But we know enough about heaven to know that it will be glorious. I believe that God has saved the best for last—heaven being the final chapter in His unfolding drama of redemption.

This was what Paul had in mind when he said of this divine drama: *"Things which eye has not seen and ear has not heard, and which have not entered the heart of man,* **all that God has prepared for those who love Him***"* (1 Corinthians 2:9). This includes heaven, but Paul is writing about God's plan of redemption that was revealed in successive stages to His people. The Old Testament saints could barely imagine what the grace of God would look like through the lens of the crucifixion of the perfect Son of God. They could only anticipate the coming of the Promised One.

But now we see the work of redemption more clearly. The volumes written about Christ's finished work on the cross stagger our imagination. That's why the preaching of the cross is so amazing. Now take this truth and compare it to all that

God is preparing for us in heaven. Yes, there is still a lot of mystery there, but it's a wonderful mystery! I makes me think of the words of the mega-popular song today, "I Can Only Imagine."

I mentioned earlier that one of the great joys of heaven is that we will have new bodies, made like Jesus' perfect, post-resurrection body, free of pain and weakness. Here is the rest of Paul's statement about our heavenly citizenship, which was briefly cited above: *"For our citizenship is in heaven, from which also we eagerly wait for a Savior, the Lord Jesus Christ; **who will transform the body of our humble state into conformity with the body of His glory**"* (Philippians 3.20–21).

Can you even begin to imagine the transformation that will happen to our bodies in heaven? People work hard and spend a lot of money to stave off the effects and appearance of aging, with only some success. But in heaven, we will be perfect. Think about that!

Before we move on, I want to give you one more passage to whet your appetite for the joys of heaven. The apostle John wrote: *"Beloved, now we are children of God, and it has not appeared as yet what we will be. We know that when He appears, we will be like Him, because we will see Him just as He is. And everyone who has this hope fixed on Him purifies himself, just as He is pure"* (1 John 3.2–3).

That last sentence gives us *the most important* element in preparing for and anticipating heaven. It's to live our lives today with our hearts purified from sin and focused on serving and glorifying the Lord.

Barriers to Anticipating Heaven

For this last essential, I'm using the word "barriers" not in the spiritual sense of failing to prepare for heaven by not trusting Christ as our Savior. That would certainly be the biggest barrier of all. Instead, I want to think with you about things that may keep us from anticipating heaven and preparing for it to make our homegoing more joyful for us and even for the loved ones we leave behind.

One big barrier to this is simply the fact that even Christians put off looking to the end of life. As I said earlier, it's just part of our humanity to want to focus on the now and push the other thoughts out there til later. And we know that many people are simply afraid to even think about death, let alone talk about it or look ahead to it.

I had a good friend in Dallas who went to be with the Lord some years ago. He had planned his memorial service, which included a ten-minute video that was played at his service. He spoke to the people gathered and to his family, and the impact was tremendous. It was a blessing to everyone, and through it, his influence carried on even from the grave.

Why don't we talk about heaven? One big reason is that people are afraid to talk about death, as we discussed in the previous essential. But for believers in Jesus Christ, death is simply the portal to heaven. The moment we close our eyes in death, we will open them in heaven and see Jesus face-to-face. That's what Paul meant when he said he would *"prefer rather to be absent from the body and to be at home with the Lord"* (2 Corinthians 5.8).

Ernest Becker wrote a Pulitzer Prize-winning book decades ago called *The Denial of Death*. We live in a culture that denies death; we want to live forever, to stay young. For many people, this life is their heaven and they don't want to leave it. They want to stay as long as they can.

It's important to consider Satan's work in this section, because in this case, too, he has a scheme to keep us focused on earth and keep our minds off of heaven. Satan knows that there is nothing he can do to rob a believer of heaven. But he knows that if he can keep us distracted with the issues of life and fearful of looking at the end of life, he can blunt our effectiveness for Christ now and rob us of the joy of anticipating eternity with Christ.

I believe Satan's number one tool to keep people in general from thinking about the end of this life and eternity is the fear of death. For people who don't know Christ, the fear of death is often very real. But even as believers, we still can experience that very human fear of death because of its finality as part of the unknown.

But we need to always remember that for the Christian, death is not an enemy to be feared any longer, but simply the necessary passageway into heaven. Paul called death *"the last enemy that will be abolished"* (1 Corinthians 15.26) when

Jesus returns and takes His people to heaven. This is one more exciting reason that we can anticipate heaven with no reservations! The writer of Hebrews celebrates this freedom from fear in a wonderful passage:

> *Therefore, since the children share in flesh and blood, He Himself likewise also partook of the same, that through death He might render powerless him who had the power of death, that is, the devil, and might free those who through fear of death were subject to slavery all their lives.* Hebrews 2.14–15

Notice that the writer doesn't say that Jesus has freed us from death, but from the *fear* of death, which is a form of slavery. Again, death is the door to heaven for Christians. In fact, we must go through this door because *"flesh and blood **cannot** inherit the kingdom of God; nor does the perishable inherit the imperishable"* (1 Corinthians 15.50). Who wants to go to heaven with these aging, aching bodies we have now? I don't! We will need new, perfect bodies to enjoy all the perfections of heaven—and I can't wait for my new body!

I love what Dr. Tony Evans said about the fear of death. He said the very thing we fear won't happen to us because the minute we close our eyes on earth, we will open them in heaven. In this same context Paul also reminds us to live well in this present life since we each will be held accountable (recompensed) for how we have lived in this life:

"Therefore, we also have as our ambition, whether at home or absent, to be pleasing to Him. For we must all appear before the judgment seat of Christ, so that each one may be recompensed for his deeds in the body, according to what he has done, whether good or bad."
2 Corinthians 5.6–10

A Closing Thought

My final encouragement to you is not to let these barriers keep you from joyfully anticipating heaven. Death is coming for all of us, just as it came for Jesus. But He conquered death and rose from the dead, and we will too! Praise God!

So let me urge you to have healthy discussions regarding the truth of heaven with your aging peers, your adult children and the generations following them. Study what God's Word has to say about heaven, and revel in its truths. There have been some great books written about heaven, and I leave you with a short, selected list:

- *Heaven*, Joseph Bayly, David C. Cook Publishers, 1977, 1987 Joe was a mentor of mine; it is one of my favorite books written about heaven.
- *Heaven*, Randy Alcorn, Tyndale House Publishers, 2004
- *50 Days of Heaven: Reflections That Bring Eternity to Light*, Randy Alcorn, 2006
- *The Dawn of Heaven Breaks, Anticipating Eternity*, Sharon James (EP books, 2016)

- *I Shall Not Die, But Live: Facing Death with Gospel Hope,* Douglas Taylor (Banner, 2016, an outstanding personal testimony)

Let me finish by asking you this all-important question. Where will you be when you are no longer here? I encourage you to make certain about your salvation. And then, as Christians like to say when parting, "I'll see you here, there, or in the air!"

A Shorter Bibliography for the Joy of Living Our Senior Years

Richard and Leona Bergstrom, *THIRD CALLING: What are you doing the rest of your life?* Re-ignite, a division of Church Health, 2016.

Jim Burns, *Doing Life with Your Adult Children: Keep Your Mouth Shut and Welcome Mat Out*, Zondervan, 2019.

L.S. Dugdale, MD, *The Lost Art of Dying: Reviving Forgotten Wisdom*, Harper One, 2020.

Alice Fryling, *Aging Faithfully: The Holy Invitation of Growing Older*, Nav Press, 2021.

John Stuart Gilbert & Robert Stuart Gilbert, *From Eden to Paradise: Something Stronger than Time*, Xulon Press, 2012.

Hal Habecker, *What the Bible Says about Growing Older: The Exciting Potential in This Season of Life*, Finishing Well Ministries, 2022.

James Houston & Michael Parker, *A Vision for the Aging Church: Renewing Ministry for and by Seniors,* IVP Academic, 2011.

J.I. Packer, *Finishing Our Course with Joy: Guidance from God for Engaging with Our Aging*, Crossway, 2014.

Bruce Peppin, *The Best Is Yet to Be: Moving Mountains in Mid-Life*, David C. Cook, 2015.

Derek Prime, *A Good Old Age: An A to Z of Loving and Following the Lord Jesus in the Later Years*, 10 Publishing, 2017.

VantagePoint3 Team, *A Mentoring Guide: Christ-Conversation-Companionship*, VantagePoint3, 2019.

Wes Wick, *Half Two: The Quest for a God-Honoring ENCORE*, Yes! Young Enough to Serve, 2017

Robert Wolgemuth, *Gunlap: Staying in the Race with Purpose*, B & H Publishing, 2021.

Robert Wolgemuth, *Finish Line: Dispelling Fear, Finding Peace, and Preparing for the End of your Life*, Zondervan, 2023.

MINISTRIES

"Fulfilling God's Plan in Our Aging Years"

"Finishing Well Ministries aims to encourage every retired Christian and every Christian thinking about retirement to understand and to fully live out God's plan for these critically important years."

For a deeper dive into the Seven Essentials for Finishing Well, see the website for a multi-part study including videos and a workbook. Do the self-study, then take the study to your community group.

www.FinishingWellMinistries.org

NOTES:

Made in the USA
Monee, IL
06 October 2025

30578001R10079